BETWEEN loyalty and disobedience; between recognition of the law's authority and realization that the law is not always right: in America, this conflict is historic, with results as glorious as the mass protests of the civil rights movement and as inglorious as the armed violence of the militia movement. In an impassioned defense of dissent, Stephen L. Carter argues for the dialogue that negotiates this conflict and keeps democracy alive. His book portrays an America dying from a refusal to engage in such a dialogue, a polity where, indeed, everybody speaks, but nobody listens.

The Dissent of the Governed is an eloquent diagnosis of what ails the body politic—the unwillingness of people in power to hear disagreement unless forced to—and a prescription for a new process of response. Carter examines the divided American political character on dissent, with special reference to religion, identifying it in unexpected places, with an eye toward amending it before it destroys our democracy.

At the heart of this work is a rereading of the Declaration of Independence that puts dissent, not consent, at the center of the question of the legitimacy of democratic government. Carter warns that our liberal constitutional ethos—the tendency to assume that the nation must everywhere be morally the same—pressures citizens to be other than themselves when being themselves would lead to disobedience. This tendency, he argues, is particularly hard on religious citizens, whose notion of community may be quite different from that of the sovereign majority of citizens. His book makes a powerful case

THE DISSENT OF THE GOVERNED

The William E. Massey Sr. Lectures in the
History of American Civilization

1995

The Dissent
of the Governed

A MEDITATION ON
LAW, RELIGION, AND LOYALTY

Stephen L. Carter

HARVARD UNIVERSITY PRESS

Cambridge, Massachusetts
London, England
1998

Library of Congress Cataloging-in-Publication Data

Carter, Stephen L., 1954–
The dissent of the governed : a meditation on law, religion, and
loyalty / Stephen L. Carter.
p. cm. — (The William E. Massey, Sr. lectures
in the history of American civilization ; 1995)
Includes bibliographical references and index.
ISBN 0-674-21265-7 (alk. paper)
1. Allegiance. 2. Government, Resistance to.
3. Religion and politics. I. Title. II. Series.
JC328.C27 1998
323.6'5—dc21
97-39973

For Harry, Guido, and Tony—all my deans—
with gratitude and affection

Contents

Preface

This book constitutes the expanded and edited text of the Massey Lectures in the History of American Civilization, delivered at Harvard University in May of 1995. I have styled the book as a meditation, because I freely confess that I continue to puzzle over the subject that occupies the lectures it contains: the relationship between loyalty and disobedience on the one hand and, on the other, between recognition of the sovereign's authority and realization that the sovereign is not always right. In America, this conflict is eternal, with results at times glorious—as in the mass protest wing of the civil rights movement—and at times tragic—as in the armed and violent wing of the militia movement.

As a legal theorist, as a citizen of a democracy, and as a Christian, I believe, deeply, in dissent, not simply as a right, but often as a responsibility. Our moral progress demands richer understandings of the world, and nobody has yet invented a better or more democratic source of those understandings than dialogue among free and equal citizens. Dialogue suggests differences of opinion; when an individual or a group differs with the opinion of the majority as reflected in law or custom, the opportunity for dissent presents itself. As the reader will quickly discover, I believe that dialogue is what the Declaration of Independence is all about, and that the refusal to engage in dialogue—most particularly when it is the state that does the refusing—is itself a manifest injustice that demands correction.

America, however, is dying from a refusal to engage in dialogue. I do not mean that nobody speaks—*everybody* speaks—but rather that nobody listens. In particular, the instrumentalities of government, especially at the national level, seem to most Americans woefully inaccessible. Both our national history and our national present teach the same lesson: people who hold power, whatever their politics, will not listen to those who disagree with them unless they are forced to. These lectures explore that aspect of the American political character, with special reference to religion, trying to illustrate it in unexpected places, as well as to help us find a path toward ameliorating it before it destroys our democracy.

Although the third lecture was substantially rewritten after delivery, I elected to make only small changes in the first two lectures, as well as in the structure of the principal argument of the entire book, prior to publication. So I must ask the reader's indulgence for my frequent references to certain momentous events—most notably the Republican landslide in the November 1994 midterm congressional election and the April 1995 bombing of the federal building in Oklahoma City—that were, at the time of the lectures, still fresh in memory. The alert reader will also notice several other stylistic fillips that may seem more appropriate to a spoken lecture than a written text.

I also beg the indulgence of readers familiar with my book *Integrity*, who have already been exposed to the story of the two liberal Christians involved with the Christian Coalition, which I discuss, from a somewhat different perspective than before, in the first lecture of the present book, and who are also familiar with my views on civil disobedience, even though I withdraw here some of what I wrote there.

Many individuals have contributed to the creation of this book. I am grateful first of all to the Program in the History of American Civilization at Harvard, and especially to Professor Alan Heimert, who extended the invitation to deliver the lectures, and was tireless and unfailingly courteous as my host in Cambridge. I benefited from the many suggestions (not all of them friendly ones) that I received from members of the audience at the time that the lectures were delivered, as well as at a faculty workshop at the Yale Law School that focused on the second lecture. I discussed the subject matter of the third lecture at workshops at the law schools of DePaul University, the University of Oklahoma, and Washington University (St. Louis), and received helpful advice on those occasions as well. Particularly helpful have been comments and proposed avenues of research from Bruce Ackerman, Akhil Amar, Robert Ellickson, Henry Louis Gates Jr., Anthony Kronman, and Kate Stith. Both the lectures and the resulting book would have been impossible without the splendid efforts of my research assistants, Deborah Baumgarten, Goodwin Liu, and Lewis Peterson, students at the Yale Law School. And, as always, I would not have been able to write a single word without the love and support of my family: my patient children, Leah and Andrew, and, most especially, my wife, Enola Aird, for whose sharp eye for the senseless sentence and for whose gifts of wisdom, guidance, and criticism I will forever be grateful.

Finally, I should note that when I chose the title *The Dissent of the Governed*, I was unaware of the fascinating 1976 book of the same name by the sociologist James D. Wright. Wright's useful contribution was to analyze—empirically as well as by other means—the extent of alienation in the United States in the late 1960s and early 1970s. He found that there was rather a lot of it, among virtually all segments of American society. I am afraid that in the twenty years since his book was published, things have just gotten worse.

S.L.C.
New Haven, Connecticut / Aspen, Colorado
July 1997

The force of a law depends on the extent of its justice.

—ST. THOMAS AQUINAS

THE DISSENT OF THE GOVERNED

I

Allegiance

M<small>Y SUBJECT</small> is the dissent of the governed. As will become clear, I am playing deliberately on Jefferson's famous language in the Declaration of Independence, in order to meditate on an aspect of our republic that we think too little about.

I want us to reflect together over these next three afternoons about the deeply rooted American tendency to dislike dissent, most notably in causes we despise. I will be speaking particularly about the ways in which whoever happens to control the apparatus of the sovereign uses its authority to manipulate both language and policy in order to make dissenters seem un-American.

In this first lecture, I will offer the justification for my inversion of our classic understanding of the Declaration of Independence, and will explore the role of religious communities in our public life, especially in education, in order to suggest how an understanding of justice as flowing not from *consent* but from our attitudes toward *dissent* might actually bind up some of the wounds from which we as a nation have bled these last few years.

In the second lecture, I will consider what happens when dissent spills over into conduct, especially conduct that happens to be illegal; and in the third lecture, I will work through the rhetoric of our constitutional courts as they deal with dissent. I should stress that in none of this is my goal principally one of law reform. I style these lectures as a meditation because I am not sure that I have answers to the problems that I am raising—and yet I am convinced that the problems are real, and will grow increasingly dangerous to our democracy if we pretend that they do not exist.

Allegiance and Democracy

A useful place to begin is with the foundational document of American history—not the Constitution, the foundational document of American law, but the Declaration of Independence. Garry Wills, in his splendid book on the document, tells us that the people who signed the Declaration paid little attention to it, considering it a relatively small bit of business, less important, for example, than the *act* of declaring independence, which took place two days earlier. This written list of grievances was principally for the purpose of convincing foreign powers to line up on the side of the Colonies rather than the side of England. The signatories, says Wills, did not believe that they were setting forth a new theory of government.[1]

Yet the writing—the act of communicating a justification—is crucial to understanding the act of declaring independence, for by offering a written argument, the leaders of the Revolution sought to provide to the world a justification for what must have seemed a foolish and headstrong move. And that writing, on a careful examination, has unavoidable implications for the subject of these lectures: the problem of dissent.

Consider what is obviously common ground. The proclamation of the Declaration was, by its terms and by its effect, an act of disallegiance, the breaking of the tie of presumptive obligation that we describe as loyalty. The argument for that act is quite famous, but bears quoting, for it actually involves a bit of a trope and hides an important point:

> We hold these truths to be self-evident, that all men are created equal, that they are endowed by their Creator with certain unalienable Rights, that among these are Life, Liberty and the pursuit of Happiness.—That to secure these rights, Governments are instituted among Men, deriving their just powers from the consent of the governed.

Let us stop there for the moment. From this quotation, certainly the best-known in the entire document, we discover that government is created in order to secure the inalienable rights

with which all people—the Declaration, of course, says "men"—
were endowed in the act of divine creation. I will return to that
point presently. For the moment, consider the final part of the
quotation. What is the source of the powers of the government? Why, "the consent of the governed," of course, the
drafters' famous appeal to the fans of Locke and Montesquieu,
who may or may not have been popular reading at the time of
the Revolution.

But did the drafters even believe this? When one reads the
list of complaints in the Declaration, one does not discover any
that have their roots in the lack of "consent" in any Lockean
sense—consent to the government apparatus—although, to be
sure, a number of them assert, in effect, a lack of consent to particular policies of the Crown. Read to the end of the Declaration, and you find what should perhaps be treated as the heart
of the matter:

> In every stage of these Oppressions We have Petitioned
> for Redress in the most humble terms: Our repeated Peti-
> tions have been answered only by repeated injury. A
> Prince, whose character is thus marked by every act which
> may define a Tyrant, is unfit to be the ruler of a free
> people.

Note where the argument is going. That the King is a tyrant
goes almost without saying. But what, in the end, makes him
tyrannical? It is not merely, perhaps not mostly, that he, in al-
liance with Parliament, has done oppressive things to the
Colonists, although that is true, and the list is quite an extensive
one. The nub of the matter, however, seems to be that he has
ignored their complaints. Listen again. We are told that the
Colonists have "Petitioned for Redress in the most humble
terms," petitions that "have been answered only by repeated injury." It seems to be the rejection of the petitions for redress—

the fact that the Crown is ignoring the particular concerns of the Colonists—that provides the justification for revolution.

Thus, the point of the Declaration seems not to celebrate the notion of *consent*, but to celebrate the notion of *dissent*. The complaint is that the Colonial acts of dissent, the articulation of the many small and large disagreements with the Crown, have fallen on deaf ears. It is not the failure of *consent* but the failure of *dissent* that has thus provided the impetus, and still more the justification, for the separation of the American colonies from the Crown, that is, for the American Revolution. True, it is consent of the governed that delivers the initial legitimacy (the "just powers") to the government. But it is the rebuffing of the "repeated Petitions" that dissolves that legitimacy.

Now, let's be careful. It is important to note that it is the sovereign's choice to ignore the petitions, not the petitions themselves, that provides the justification for the act of disallegiance. In other words, it is the Crown's treatment of the dissenters— not the fact of their dissent—that turns out to be crucial.

If this analysis is accurate, then we can say that under our reconstructed Declaration of Independence, if the sovereign repeatedly ignores and rebuffs the complaints of its subjects—or, nowadays, its citizens—the sovereign will lose their allegiance. Because whatever may be the significance of the allegiance of an individual to a sovereign, the individual surely expects a modicum of respect and attention in return.

Let me emphasize that I am not, yet, making an argument about political theory. I am making an argument about practical politics—a practical politics that the drafters of the Declaration of Independence perfectly well understood. The practical political point is this: whatever may be the source of the sovereign's theoretical legitimacy, that legitimacy may vanish if "repeated Petitions" for "Redress" are, in the eyes of the citizenry, "answered only by repeated injury."

6

Now, what happens when we transfer this argument across some two centuries and more since the signing of the Declaration? What happens is this: we can look around the United States and see a nation in which large numbers of citizens do indeed feel that their petitions to their government go unanswered, and, as a result, have lost a degree of their faith in that government. Does this mean that they are also losing their allegiance? That, it seems to me, is by far the most crucial question for everyone who is concerned about the future of the American democracy. And it is the question that will occupy me in this first lecture.

Disallegiance and Democracy

As we struggle toward the end of the twentieth century, the mightiest, wealthiest, and most envied nation on the face of the planet, surveys tell us that four out of five Americans believe that something has gone terribly wrong with our society, that we have somehow jumped the track. But what? Let me offer some possibilities.

I have spent much time recently traveling to different parts of the country and talking to audiences, many of them deeply religious, about the intersection of law and politics. The mood I have found has been depressing. I pride myself on being the world's worst political prognosticator, but in the early fall of 1994, I began to tell my friends and colleagues that the people I was meeting on my sojourns were so upset, so mistrustful of government, that the elections were going to turn the country upside down. For once, it seems, I was right.

There is, I suppose, no consensus on precisely what terribly wrong direction the nation has taken, but it is plain from the surveys and from the phenomenal growth in conservative religious organizations—as well as from my conversations with the people I have been meeting—that much of the concern focuses on questions of morality. The sense, in other words, is that it is the nation's *values* that have gone off the track.

This sense is particularly strong among socially conservative religious communities, principally the Evangelical faiths and Roman Catholics. (I include among these socially conservative religions the strong black church tradition, whose adherents tend to be, on nearly every moral issue, well to the right of the American political mean.) Nowadays, these communities are marked by a yearning for morality, both in the sense of a set of values connected to their particular religious traditions, and in the different but of course related sense of simply wanting to live in a society that talks seriously about standards of conduct, about right and wrong—and, by extension, a society in which citizens who choose to talk seriously about right and wrong are not treated as outcasts.

This concern crosses into politics, and although secular liberals often do not like it, there is no choice but to accept it. Such groups as Christian Coalition, the Traditional Values Coalition, Concerned Women for America, and Excellence in Education number their members in the millions. Nobody challenges the figures. These and similar groups attack a secular morality that, as they describe it, celebrates the self, insists on the relativism of values, and maligns the nation's religious traditions. One need not agree with their social critique or their program to appreciate their appeal.

The appeal, moreover, crosses political lines. Bill Clinton won the presidency in 1992 and again in 1996 as a New Democrat, and liberals who yearn for the old kind would do well to recall that since 1964, *every* elected president has been either a conservative Republican or a Southern Democrat. At some point, one must concede that there is more going on than coincidence. And one of the things that is going on is that the

American voters seem most ready to cede the bully pulpit of the presidency to people who they believe will speak in the language of right and wrong. Sometimes, the people are more ready to do this than to cast their votes for another candidate who might, on the issues, be more in tune with their views.

One reason for this is that most Americans describe themselves as religious; and for most religious people, religion matters. It is difficult sometimes for secular liberals to imagine that there are people to whom faith is more important than particular political ends, but in fact there are many. In my travels, I have met self-described political liberals who are members of, or sympathetic with, such groups as Christian Coalition, simply because they do not feel that liberal organizations respect their religiosity. I often tell the story of meeting two black women who moved from involvement in liberal politics to involvement in conservative Christian groups for no other reason than their perception that, among their natural liberal political allies, their desire to talk about their faith—evangelical Christianity—made them an object of sport. Choosing between possible homes, then, they preferred a place that honored their faith and disdained their politics over a place that honored their politics and disdained their faith.

Their story is a tragedy, but it is one that is repeated across the country. Mainstream politics, with its arrogant rejection of religious argument and traditional religious values, has alienated tens of millions of voters, and by no means are all of them hard-line conservatives. You will note that I use the term "politics"—not "liberalism"—because even though, as will be seen, liberalism bears some of the blame, the dominant political ethos is complicated. And the very complication of contemporary government makes matters worse. In nearly every community I visit, I find people who believe that they live in a system in which vital decisions are made in far-off Washington by faceless and often nameless bureaucrats who care nothing for them or their values. And the anger at Washington as an entity can trump all other concerns. One woman in a small town near Harrisburg told me that she is not against school lunch programs, she just doesn't trust "Washington" to administer them—or, perhaps more to the point, she is angry because she does not feel that "Washington" trusts her.[2]

That is the frightening way people talk about the nation's capital nowadays, using the name of the city as though it has a malevolent sentience of its own. Washington, where the federal government sits. Washington, which doesn't care and doesn't listen. You can almost hear the echoes of the language of the Declaration of Independence. Listen again: "In every stage of these Oppressions We have Petitioned for Redress in the most humble terms: Our repeated Petitions have been answered only by repeated injury." That is why I worry that the country is in the throes of a massive act of disallegiance, of which the 1994 elections were but the merest spasm.

Now, do not misunderstand me. I am not talking about the members of the nation's burgeoning militia movement, or the people who tune in to hear talk radio hosts advising them to shoot federal agents in the head because they will be wearing bullet-proof vests. And, God knows, I am not talking about the vicious and soulless murders of the innocent that we witnessed in the bombing of the federal building in Oklahoma City in April of 1995. I am not, in other words, talking about violence (although I will have something to say about it in the second lecture). I am talking about ordinary, hard-working, law-abiding families, patriotic Americans whose political allegiance to the nation runs deep and whose moral roots are in their religious traditions, to which their allegiance runs just as deep; families who are concerned, frightened, and, more and more, profoundly alienated from politics and from a government that they think does not care about them.

Of particular concern to the members of these communities is the moral upbringing of the young. Once upon a time, it was said that values climbed from one generation to the next on a three-legged stool. The three legs were the home, the school, and the place of worship. Should any one of the three legs break, so the story went, the stool would topple and the values would not be passed on. And were that to happen, the traditions that generated the values would simply cease to exist.

That is precisely the situation in which many religious people believe they live. It does not matter whether one agrees with them, either on the way values are transmitted or on whether the stool has broken. I am trying to explain the perception. Again and again in my travels, I run into people who complain that the deck is stacked against a family trying to teach what they often call "traditional values" or "family values." Many of these traditional values, of course, deal with sexual behavior, which is unsurprising, because the cabining of sexuality has long been of vital concern to the Judeo-Christian tradition. But of course these traditional values may also include everything from an obligation to feed the hungry to the importance of discipline and persistence. Now, I am neither defending nor criticizing the values they have in mind; indeed, for present purposes, the values scarcely matter, except that none of the people to whom I am referring strike me as bigots or fanatics who want to train their children as fascists. My point is that there is a widely shared perception that the institutions of the government, far from reinforcing the values many people want their children to learn, actively frustrate them.

The complaints focus on politics, on the media, and on that arch-villain, the Supreme Court. But most of the complaints that I hear are in one way or another about the schools. It is not simply a matter of religious parents who want their children out of the sex education curriculum or who worry about the strange ideas in the books that are assigned. A far broader segment of the public is worried about the schools, a sentiment that is captured in the overwhelming popular support for organized classroom prayer. Now, I happen to be a skeptic of public school prayer, although I will not here burden you with the reasons.[3] But the strong majority that favors it evidently believes that students who pray in school will grow into more moral adults.

I am not here concerned with whether this prediction is true. What is more important is that school prayer is, for many parents, a symbol of a different way of life—a way of life that they want for their children and that they believe is denied to them by an uncaring authority, an authority that treats their desire to raise their children in a particular religious tradition as irrelevant or even dangerous. We talk a great deal about the stultifying effects of forcing people into religious observances, and we are right to have that worry; coercion of faith is both immoral and unconstitutional. But we sometimes miss, in our rush to celebrate our own open-mindedness, the way that a strongly secular bias can be equally stultifying to people whose religious faith is at the center of their lives.[4] To tell people whose faith influences their values that there is something wrong with those values is to tell them that there is something wrong with their faith. For tens of millions of Americans, faith in God *is* central to existence, so central that there is no sphere of life in which acknowledgment of that faith is deemed inappropriate. This, I fear, is just one of several aspects of life in much of America that too many of the American people think their government either fails to understand or actively rejects.

Very well, many people feel stifled, especially by some aspects of the system of public education. They even feel, in the sense of the Declaration of Independence, that their "repeated Petitions" are being rebuffed. The question, then, is whether this can be said to affect their allegiance to the nation—that is, whether their alienation, their sense of isolation, of a government that does not care, somehow creates conditions in which a statement of disallegiance is comprehensible or indeed likely.

Allegiance and Will

Let us think for a moment about allegiance. Not about the more familiar topic of loyalty, but about allegiance itself, the form of commitment that makes loyalty possible.

Allegiance may be willed. Probably it should be willed, for actual consent is obviously superior to tacit consent. If an allegiance is an act of will, then it is the fruit of a decision, and the very word "decision," as the theologian Margaret Farley reminds us, means, quite literally, "cutting away."[5] Thus to *decide* is to *cut away other possibilities*, a process that Christian ethics has always treated as liberating, even though in our era of celebration of the self, we tend to see only its limits. And to decide on an allegiance—to *will* an allegiance—is, by definition, to deny, to cut away, other allegiances that are possible and yet inconsistent.

In the United States, a willed allegiance is required only of immigrants seeking to become citizens. They must take instruction in the country's history and government structure and then take oaths to support the laws of the nation. So why not require that all Americans, upon reaching mature age, take oaths of loyalty prior to entering upon the privileges and obligations of full citizenship? In theory, this practice would dispense with the tricky problem of tacit consent, and would also more firmly knit us into a single national community. But even if one concedes that a national community is in fact desirable, our history teaches us to be suspicious of the loyalty oath, and our recent constitutional jurisprudence, for better or worse, teaches that an oath cannot be imposed.

The Supreme Court's decisions about loyalty oaths are interpretations of the First Amendment,[6] but the notion that the
freedom of speech denies the state the opportunity to insist on
the allegiance of its citizens is no more than slightly plausible.
As Peter Schuck and Rogers Smith point out, a better place to
look for the reason that loyalty oaths are not allowed is the Citizenship Clause of the Fourteenth Amendment.[7] In that clause,
a Congress sensitive to the efforts of the southern states to deny
the citizenship of the recently freed slaves provided that "All
persons born or naturalized in the United States, and subject to
the jurisdiction thereof, are citizens of the United States and of
the State wherein they reside." This language does not necessarily ban loyalty oaths, but it makes a ban more plausible.

Of course, once one leaves the level of political governance,
most of the allegiances that we enjoy *are* willed. We join clubs
and professional organizations and civic associations out of
choice. And religious communities, even if they begin socializ-
ing their members in childhood, usually expect, at an appropriate moment, a more mature commitment to the life of faith in
the tradition. In some Christian traditions, for example, this
might involve the affirmation of the baptismal covenant when a
young adult makes what is called a confirmation.

But perhaps the most obvious example of an allegiance that is
willed is marriage, in which wife and husband join in a ceremony that might seem, on somber reconsideration, startlingly
elaborate; but it is elaborate for a reason. The formalistic and
formulaic nature of the wedding vow (no matter which one)
marks the event and the concomitant promise as radically different from other allegiances that one might pledge. And if the
married couple is blessed with children, the marriage relationship, with all of its complexities and interlocking obligations,
becomes the even more radically distinct relationship of family.

But political allegiances are, for most Americans, never willed.

The fact of a political allegiance does mean that one acknowledges, perhaps tacitly, the legitimacy of a political sovereign, be it located in Washington, the state capital, the town hall, or even the headquarters of the school district. We do not, as a rule, select these allegiances, except in the sense that we may move from one state to another or from one school district to another. We know that when we move to a new state, we must obey that state's laws, and thus should inform ourselves on their content—Is the speed limit on highways 55 or 65? What is the sales tax? How does one register to vote?—but this is not the same as saying that we recognize our move itself as a transference of allegiance: "Yesterday I was a loyal citizen of California. Today I am a loyal citizen of New York."

Yet nobody seriously questions that we owe allegiance to the sovereign anyway. Political theory is full of explanations for the allegiance that an individual owes to his or her community (and the limits of that allegiance), and I will not review them here. But it is useful to note that communities in their actual operation tend to assume entitlement to the allegiance of their members, that no argument from justice is necessary; what communities demand instead is a justification for the counterallegiance that they owe to their members. In other words, communities as they seem to function do not begin, as political theory does, by asking what justifies the commands of the sovereign; and they often punish harshly those who seek answers to those very questions.

Communities tend to behave this way even in their formation. The United States of America was scarcely a decade old when it enacted the Sedition Acts, which were immediately applied as a political tool for the silencing of dissent. Among the dominant Federalists, there was no serious issue of the constitutional, to say nothing of the moral, validity of the legislation. Nor was any concern raised about the reasons that anybody ought to obey. The shoe was very much on the other foot: it was the dissenters and critics, not the state, not the political sovereign, that owed an explanation.

The nation, moreover, has behaved in this manner through every era of its history. Whether the forces of reaction or progress have been ascendant, whoever has held the levers of power has simply presumed an entitlement to use them, and has treated those in dissent as obviously wrong and even disloyal. Even though we have tried nobody for treason since World War II,[8] we have developed an entire rhetoric of what we seem to consider its functional equivalents, from the "Un-American Activities" investigations of the 1950s and early 1960s to the "Love It or Leave It" slogans of the Vietnam era to the familiar charges today that one or another conservative organization plans to "undermine our fundamental rights." And if one set of slogans was pioneered by the right and another by the left, that is only evidence that charging others with disloyalty is a phenomenon of the possession of political power, not the exclusive property of one corner of the political spectrum. Thus for whatever movement holds sway over the apparatus of the secular sovereign, loyalty is defined as allegiance and, all too often, allegiance as agreement; to dispute the political program of the moment is to be un-American. It is as though we have forgotten the advice of James Madison in *Federalist No. 10*, that "the first object of government" is to protect our ability to reach different conclusions, because the alternative is to create a society in which every citizen holds "the same opinions, the same passions, and the same interests."

Now, I do not want to press this point too far. Obviously, a civic community cannot survive in a constant state of dissensus. Civic life requires dissent because it requires differences of opinion in order to spark the dialogues from which the community thrives and grows. But not all the dissent—indeed, as little of it as possible—can go to the very legitimacy of the political community itself. Thus the political community must be able to distinguish between disagreement with particular policies of the community and disloyalty to the community itself.

Sometimes we are able to make this distinction. But too often, on the issues that fire the greatest controversy, we are not: instead, we adopt a rhetorical style in which dissent *is* treated as disloyalty, and disloyalty as an act of disallegiance, needing a justification. Here our own history only embarrasses us: the Declaration of Independence, if put to a vote as a text, would almost certainly be voted down. And the grievances of the Colonists seem rather thin when placed against the legitimate anger of, say, African Americans or Native Americans of today. (One of the enduring curiosities of our contemporary debate on affirmative action is the unwillingness of opponents to concede the *moral* claim of the proponents, whatever they think of the strategy: that is, to say yes, the nation does owe a moral debt to those it has so long punished on account of color, so let us debate the form that the discharge of that debt should take.)

But let us not be distracted. More to the point, even when a justification for an act of disallegiance is offered, it is bound to be rejected: no political sovereign could long survive were it to allow disallegiance of the many communities that it comprises. King George understood this point, and so made war on the Colonies after they declared their independence. Abraham Lincoln repeatedly cited the same concern as he prosecuted the bloody war against the rebellious South. The Union, he insisted, was indissoluble, and had to act to preserve itself against those who claimed otherwise. Even Dwight Eisenhower, when he sent troops to Little Rock in 1958 to enforce the Supreme Court's desegregation decrees, was acting, in the end, from a kind of inevitability: as the head of the executive branch of the political sovereign, he could not countenance the open challenge to that sovereignty that was posed by the segregationist defiance.

And yet this bit of political reality does nothing to overcome the challenge posed by our reinterpretation of the Declaration of Independence. If a community believes that it has genuine grievances against the political sovereign, and if its "repeated Petitions" to that sovereign are rebuffed, or, worse, answered with "repeated injury," does there come a point when the community's allegiance to the sovereign, no matter how formed, can fairly be said to be dissolved? In contemporary America, this is no idle question, for the nation is all too full of people and groups who insist that the political sovereign does not hear their voices. It is these groups, alienated from mainstream politics and from their government, whose disaffection may turn to disallegiance; and it is our ability to prevent that disallegiance without resort to widespread violence that will test whether we have learned as much as we smugly think we have since July of 1776.

President Clinton, in his graduation address at Michigan State University in May of 1995, criticized the contemporary militia movement for making any pretense of a continuity with the Founding Generation. He vigorously disputed the notion that one can be a loyal American without being loyal to the government—in our terms, the constituted political sovereign—and he warned that violence is never justified in pressing a grievance against the state.

Although I share the President's opposition to the militias, I am not sure that I agree with him on the issue of violence, at least not in all circumstances. The Oklahoma City bombing that generated his remarks was an unforgivable act of wanton slaughter, as nearly all political violence is, especially in a democracy. But I think I would be prepared to say that the enslaved peoples of the antebellum South, on the relatively rare occasions that they undertook acts of violent rebellion, had ample justification for doing so. Let me put to one side, however, the problem of violence, which I will take up in the second lecture.

Liberal Constitutionalism

Some of the reasons for the sense of alienation I have described are familiar, or should be: significant economic dislocations as the labor market undergoes radical changes; the nation's tilt away from its towns (and lately its cities) as it settles into middle-class suburban consumerist complacency; and the depressing persistence of both crime and poverty, two obviously related phenomena that refuse to disappear, no matter how many wars are declared on either one. And then there are what have come to be called the social issues, many of which boil down to a battle between ways of looking at the world, one deeply secular and pressing for change, the other deeply religious and tied to tradition.

I will have more to say of that battle in a moment. First, I would like to take a moment to make some enemies now by suggesting that a large part of the problem is the project of liberal constitutionalism. But before you bristle, let me explain what I mean. By the project of liberal constitutionalism, I mean the effort to use the power of the federal government, and to interpret the Constitution, in a way that creates a single, nationwide community with shared values and shared, enforceable understandings of how local communities of all descriptions should be organized.

The project of liberal constitutionalism is aimed at enabling all citizens to enjoy a set of rights both defined and enforced by the apparatus of the national government. Described this way—and the description is entirely fair—I would have to say that I find myself largely in sympathy. Except that what I suspect I am actually in sympathy with is not the notion of a single national community, but a particular vision of rights that I hope that the national sovereign will enforce.

This point bears emphasis. The liberal constitutional project is in a powerful sense anti-democratic, and it is certainly anti-communitarian. The goal of the project is to get the answers right, not to worry too much about the process through which the answers are obtained. The project, moreover, is built on a model holding that the central government (where decisions on matters of right and wrong are made) is more likely than anybody else to find the answers that are right. Thus, if it is important that women have the right to reproductive privacy— that is, the abortion right—then it does not really matter, in the larger project, whether that right stems from the due process clause of the Fourteenth Amendment (as the Supreme Court held in *Roe v. Wade*)[9] or the freedom of religion clause of the First Amendment (as Ronald Dworkin and others have proposed)[10] or some other source. Indeed, in the end, it scarcely matters whether the right is protected by the Constitution or by legislation. And certainly the views of the American people are irrelevant, except when they happen to be in support, in which case they are crucial. What matters is that the right exist and that its contents be the same everywhere.

That is why decisions like *Planned Parenthood of Southeastern Pennsylvania v. Casey*,[11] a 1992 case in which the Supreme Court allowed the states to place some restrictions on the abortion right, are so bitterly attacked by mainstream scholars: if the states can place limits on the right, then the contents of the right are not the same everywhere, and the single-community project is endangered.

But because the liberal constitutional project has been obsessed with making sure that the national sovereign reaches the right decisions, it has largely ignored the problem of placing structural limits on the powers of that national sovereign. The concern of liberal constitutionalism has been that the national sovereign (and the local sovereigns) not violate any individual's "fundamental rights," a phrase that might sound like the language of natural law but is, in practice, the language of positivism, for it is always used, by scholars and judges alike, to speak of rights that are purportedly found in the document itself. When a fundamental right is violated, liberal constitutionalism says the sovereign has overreached. But absent such a violation, the liberal constitutional project has treated the national sovereign as plenary in its authority.

That is why, when the Supreme Court occasionally reminds the executive and legislative branches that the text of the Constitution seems to contemplate the exercise of power according to a particular set of procedures, scholars (and dissenting Justices) rush to condemn the decisions as "formalistic" or "sterile." So when the Justices hold unconstitutional such innovations as the legislative veto,[12] defenders of federal power tend to scoff. The Justices, we are told, are being backward again; they are failing to understand, it seems, the needs of a modern and sophisticated state.

Viewed against the backdrop of the general project of liberal constitutionalism, this criticism makes a good deal of sense, for that project, perhaps since *McCulloch v. Maryland*[13] in 1819, and certainly since the New Deal, has treated the exercise of federal power as essentially plenary, restrained not by the formalities of process, but only by the assertion of rights. *McCulloch*, you will recall, sustained the congressional establishment of the Bank of the United States even in the absence of an express constitutional grant of power to the Congress to establish one. And during the New Deal, the Supreme Court rapidly retreated from a narrow reading of the power of the Congress to a very broad one, permitting the establishment of the vast federal administrative apparatus that seems ever since to have grown from day to day.[14] So when in April of 1995 the Court, by a narrow margin, astonished the legal world by holding that the Congress had no power to regulate the carrying of handguns near public schools,[15] we were treated once more to the vision of the Justices as troglodytes.

Liberal constitutionalism has abandoned the understanding of the Enlightenment liberals that government authority itself posed a problem for the freedom of the individual, and that the sovereign therefore had to be constrained, its powers divided. The Founders certainly understood the point, as even a cursory reading of *The Federalist* makes clear. But nowadays that vision has collapsed. The protection of the individual is not the limits on government power, but the possession of rights. At the same time, as the interests of that national sovereign have expanded, the nation as a whole has adapted to at least this corner of liberal ideology, so that few Americans seem to consider the federal government to be a government of limited, delegated powers. What this change in the understanding of national governance overlooked, and what events have now taught, is the possibility that the awesome and structurally uncheckable power of the national sovereign that liberal constitutionalism has constructed might fall into the hands of political movements working in pursuit of goals quite inimical to the political program of liberal politics. If that should happen—and some would say it has already happened—the liberal constitutional project has effectively stripped local political sovereigns of the structural ability to resist the national sovereign's decrees.

The legal academy, with visible reluctance, is coming to recognize this failing. For example, Richard Delgado and Jean Stefancic have pointed out the way that the liberal constitutional project of sameness is beginning to backfire in the quest for at least some versions of equality: "Today, for the first time in half a century, large groups of people (e.g., the State of Colorado) behave according to a lower standard than do individuals or small cities (e.g., Boulder, Aspen or Denver). By the same token, the national government and Supreme Court are becoming less receptive to minority concerns than their state or local counterparts."[16] A word of explanation is in order. The authors' reference in discussing Colorado is to the state's controversial effort, approved by a majority of voters, to preempt local gay rights ordinances.[17] The reference to the national government and Supreme Court is principally to efforts in Washington, D.C., both legislative and judicial, to overturn affirmative action plans adopted by local non-federal government entities. And although I am not sure that the authors have their history right—in the realm of religious oppression, for example, what they describe has been the rule, not the exception—they are struggling toward a celebration of community, in the sense of geographic localism, that the liberal constitutional project largely forbids.

An important focus of their analysis is the Supreme Court's 1989 decision in *City of Richmond v. J. A. Croson*,[18] which held unconstitutional the "minority set-aside" plan for public contracts adopted by the Richmond city council. Of *Croson*, the authors say this: "Richmond's own interpretation of its regional history, customs, and culture, which dictated a remedy for the lack of black contractors and builders, was overridden in favor of a sterile neutralism."[19] The principal opposition that the authors try to create—a sensitive interpretation against a sterile neutralism—is not the important one. The opposition that matters is the one that is captured in a single word of their critique. That word is *overridden*. Thus the question they perhaps ought to ask is this one: By what authority does the national community override this or any judgment of the local community?

One answer that is easy—and true—is that we fought the

Civil War to resolve that question. Another answer that is easy—and true—is that whatever the Civil War left unresolved we settled in 1958, when President Eisenhower sent troops to Little Rock to enforce the Supreme Court's judgment in *Cooper v. Aaron*,[20] a pivotal desegregation decision that expressly denied any privilege of local governments to interpret the Constitution differently from the way that the Supreme Court interprets it. Indeed, one of the most vivid images in the legal history of the civil rights movement—aside from the heroic lawyers who argued the cases—is the image of the fifty-eight heroic federal judges in the South who enforced desegregation decrees in the face of popular opposition and very real threats to their safety.

But I wonder now, looking back, whether our reverence for those judges for standing firm—and for the national government over the states—is not simply an artifact of which power was on which side. I suspect that our love for federal power is really a love for the formal equality rules that federal power was able to produce. And if we take a moment to think counter-historically, and imagine a national sovereign in the 1950s under the control of the southern segregationists and trying to force Jim Crow on a resisting North, I doubt that our image today of the relative benevolence of the two powers, the state and the federal, would be the same.

The 1950s are, however, the crucial era in evaluating the relationship of federalism to the liberal constitutional project. The reason is that contrary to the ringing rhetoric of many a scholar, the vision of the nation as a single community with a single moral understanding did not really triumph at Appomattox in 1865, as the subsequent century or more of African-American suffering attests. If one must select a historical moment, one would have to say that the doctrine was established, if at all, at Little Rock in 1958.

Our historical memory of the "states' rights" claim has grown so revisionist that we see it only as a device invented to aid the oppression of African Americans. We remember, quite naturally, the attempted secession of the southern states that brought about the Civil War. We forget that the northern states had long pretended to the same rights, for example by claiming the right to nullify—that is, deny legal effect to—the Embargo Act of 1807. Indeed, even over the issue of slavery, the northern states tried to assert their independent sovereignty. In the 1840s, the Whig political leaders of the Commonwealth of Massachusetts took extraordinary measures to avoid losing the state to secessionists protesting enforcement of the Fugitive Slave Law.[21]

Of course, time quite famously marches on, and if federalism is indeed dead, perhaps it is deservedly dead—but not because it was misused as a shield for racist oppression. Its death as a significant legal doctrine was probably inevitable in the twentieth century as the population grew more mobile and the states began to lose a degree of regional diversity; and certainly it would have died in the last few decades as the mass media of communication succeeded in the work of transforming us, in several senses, into a single national community.[22]

Although surveys continue to pick up regional differences on a variety of issues, the state lines themselves remain as largely arbitrary boundaries, respected principally because they have always been respected, and we, in our national conservatism, are not swift to change. This, perhaps, is the message that we missed in the Lani Guinier contretemps early in 1993. Guinier, a law professor nominated by President Clinton to run the civil rights division of the Justice Department, was skewered by her opponents in part for her racial essentialism: she seemed to assume that black voters, for example, shared a common interest distinct from that of white voters, and only expressible through the device of black-majority districts. But as Guinier herself pointed out in one little-noted article, the idea that black voters might share a common interest is not, on its face, stranger than the idea that all the voters in a particular geographic area might share one.[23]

Still, we are wedded to our geographic districts, part of our peculiar inheritance from English practice. No more than a handful of democracies elect their legislatures through single-member districts according to the principle of winner-take-all, and no serious student of voting believes the practice an efficient means for aggregating preferences. What most democratic nations use instead is some form of proportional representation, which Guinier—but hardly Guinier alone—fervently advocated. The refusal of Guinier's critics to treat the idea with the seriousness that it deserves is evidence of the desperation with which we cling to the fiction of what I suppose we must call geographic essentialism.

Yet, as we have already observed, few Americans feel an allegiance to their state sovereigns in the same sense in which they feel an allegiance to the national sovereign. Nobody, to my knowledge, opens the school day with a pledge of allegiance to the flag of Connecticut, or Kansas, or California. Indeed, even though the Fourteenth Amendment provides for citizenship in a state as well as citizenship in the United States, few of us probably think of ourselves as state citizens. We tend to refer to ourselves instead as American citizens who are *residents* of particular states. In other words, at the level of state government, not even the voters on whose behalf the fiction of geographic essentialism is so vigorously maintained actually seem to believe it.

However one resolves that question, the larger problem should by now be clear: given a liberal constitutional regime that insists on a single set of national values, resident in fundamental law, and given the collapse of local political sovereigns as functioning intermediaries, how are we to preserve religions and other communities that offer distinct visions of the world and thus desire to dissent—or are they to be preserved at all? How, in other words, is the project of our reinterpreted Declaration of Independence—*the dissent of the governed*—to fit in with the project of liberal constitutionalism?

The Preservation of Tradition

Thus far, I have used the term "community" in its ordinary sense, denoting a geographic location, a spot on the map; and so, when I have referred to people as members of communities, I have had reference, as one might expect, to where they live. But now I want to redefine the term I have been using.

I want now to think not of a geographic community but of a community of meaning: a group of people, voluntarily associated with each other, struggling to make sense of the world. We can refer to such a community as self-defining or self-constituted, not in the sense that its members constantly reinvent themselves—although indeed they might do so—but in the sense that the community, as it struggles against the world for meaning, is defining itself according to a set of understandings that might be radically different from those that motivate the larger society in which it is embedded. Our most common experience of such communities is with the religions, which embed themselves in narrative traditions that provide meanings that enrich the lives and the very souls of the faithful, even though outsiders might find them obscure. This aspect of the religions, as the theologian David Tracy has pointed out, renders them potentially subversive: for the meanings that they discover and assign to the world may be radically distinct from those that are assigned by the political sovereign.[24] If by the nourishing strength that members draw from the community, the faithful are thus moved to dissent, we face, simultaneously, a crisis for the authority of the political sovereign and the opportunity for a dialogue that may in rare cases persuade a majority of fellow citizens that the sovereign is wrong and the dissenting religionist right.

Nowadays, the concerns perhaps most likely to fire the self-defining community are concerns about what we loosely call morality, in the sense of an "ought." A strangely surviving strand in our philosophy, derived of course from Hume, holds that it is not possible to infer an *ought* from an *is*—that is, that one cannot, through knowledge of the facts alone, determine a proper course of action. The natural law tradition, by contrast, holds that it is possible to deduce oughts from facts of at least one kind: facts about human nature. This means, of course, that the natural law tradition only works if one believes in the existence of human nature, but that is, for present purposes, a moot point. The more important point is that many religious traditions are certain that they *do* possess facts about human nature. And it is that certainty that fires the religious dimension of contemporary moral debates over issues ranging from human sexuality to human generosity.

Our most famous progressive examples of this subversive aspect of the religions are the abolitionist movement and the civil rights movement, both of which were largely inspired by the shared meanings of religious communities that were sharply different from the meanings that the larger society in those days proposed; both of which changed the nation quite radically for the better; and both of which give the lie to the constitutional canard that there is something wrong, or even something suspicious, about religious argument in American public life. Had the nation tried to enforce in the 1860s or the 1960s the depressing rules for public dialogue that liberals too often endorse today, our history—certainly my history, as an African American—would have been radically different... for the worse.

True, it is often said to be hornbook constitutional law that a religious community cannot use the coercive apparatus of the state to impose its moral understandings on those in the political community who are not co-religionists. But as many observers (myself included) have pointed out, this is not a fair description of our constitutional inheritance.[25] If it is, then either the Constitution is wrong or the *Reverend* Martin Luther King Jr., leader of the Southern *Christian* Leadership Conference, was a dangerous religious fanatic whose words and work should have been condemned by liberalism. But even if I am wrong and this description of our constitutional inheritance is right, it restricts, at most, the ability of religious communities to impose their moral truths on others—it says nothing about the ability of those communities to impose those truths on their own members.

The point is a more difficult one than might be supposed, for the project of liberal constitutionalism often places significant obstacles in the path of a religious community's ability to project its truths, or even to nurture its own existence—and the spiritual life of its adherents—over time. In particular, the liberal constitutionalist understanding of the limits on sovereign authority already threatens the autonomy of a religion as a community of meaning, because it possesses neither power, because it is not a political sovereign, nor rights, because it is not an individual.

The distinction matters. Religious communities often exert a measure of sovereign-like authority over aspects of the lives of their members. One need not agree with my view that this sovereign-like authority is often a good thing to understand that the religions do demand forms of allegiance and thus of loyalty. Sometimes the demand is aspirational—*it is better to do x rather than y*—and sometimes it flows from a religion's hierarchical organization—*you are required to do x rather than y*. The generally unfounded fear that most religions are hierarchical in the strong sense—that the faithful will do as the clergy command—underlies a significant part of the liberal opposition to religious activism in politics.

I should add that the liberal opposition to religious activism in politics is another cause of citizen alienation from government, for many deeply religious citizens do not understand how a nation can call itself democratic when they are accepted in politics only if they are willing to leave behind that aspect of their lives that provides meaning and hope. Indeed, the insistence that the faithful remake themselves before they can come before the bar of politics might seem to be a classic example of the rejection of the "repeated Petitions" of the citizenry.

Religions matter. A substantial majority of religious people tell pollsters that they consult their religious understandings as they ponder difficult moral decisions. Nearly half of religious people say that they consider the teachings of their religions when called upon to cast a vote. And the vast majority of religious adults surely want their children to grow up to be religious adults—preferably adherents to the same religious tradition as their parents.

Indeed, someone once said that our children are the people we have religions *for*, meaning that a principal purpose of religious narrative and religious observance is to preserve the tradition of the past and project it into the future. From time to time I come across critiques of religion as providing a way for parents to indoctrinate their children with superstitions; religious communities are often described as totalizing.

Outsider opinions such as these only increase the sense of alienation that I have mentioned and, no matter what the outsider may think, to the insider the task of preserving the tradition is often the crucial work of the family. I am quite firmly of the view that the religious freedom of the family to make religious decisions, including decisions on behalf of the children, is a freedom older than the Constitution, older than the earliest version of the social contract, and a freedom, therefore, with which the secular sovereign cannot interfere. So if a religious community chooses to continue its narrative through its children, that is not the business of any outsider; the outsider, after all, will likely have an entirely distinct set of epistemic premises, and thus can only blunder.

Alasdair MacIntyre has argued that traditions are simply arguments extended over history,[26] but I think Samuel Fleischacker has correctly spotted the paradox in this view: "[T]raditions are first and foremost the sum total of what is *not* argued in the transmission of knowledge and practice from parents to their children."[27] A tradition, in other words, is less an argument than an attempt to avoid an argument. It is an attempt to establish something as given—and then to use that *givenness* as a basis on which to build or maintain community, and to preserve the community's narrative into the next generation.

There are other communities, non-religious ones, that also try to establish meanings, and sometimes even make demands of loyalty on their members. The legal philosopher George Fletcher, citing the demands of solidarity by members of many groups of "hyphenated Americans," points out the way that more and more communities are coming to mimic the sovereign's narrative, in which the choice is between loyalty and treason: "We are witnessing . . . increasing demands for loyalty within smaller and smaller units of group identification."[28] I do not want to diminish in any way the felt needs of many groups for member loyalty, but I sometimes worry that our valuable contemporary celebration of multiculturalism tends to obscure the existence in our midst of communities in which traditions, transmitted over time as culture, as history, even as law, are not

merely the community's base, but the community's very definition. For religious communities in which ritual and activity are
as important as belief, the old saw remains both accurate and
valuable: We are what we do.

In a nation devoted to religious freedom, the what-we-do of
a religious community will often challenge our national understanding not only of what activities individuals may engage in,
but, indeed, of what constitutes religion itself. Surely it was
only the Supreme Court of the United States that had trouble
finding a religious freedom issue when the Air Force forbade
an officer who was an Orthodox Jew to wear his yarmulke while
in uniform[29] . . . or when the Forest Service allowed a lumber
company to cut down a forest that was crucial to a Native American religious tradition, thus causing the religion to cease to exist.[30] Such court decisions as these (and there are many, many,
far too many others, which I and others have unhappily can-
vassed elsewhere) illustrate the totalizing potentialities of liberal constitutionalism. There is little space for the construction
of communities of meaning, when that meaning is different
from the meanings of the sovereign. A forest is just a forest, not
a place of worship, say the Justices; indeed, as they point out
with something bordering on contempt, the tribes involved in
the case do not even own the land! And as for the yarmulke,
well, nobody is forcing the fellow to join the Air Force—so the
Justices reason—and once he is there, why, he has to follow the
same rules as everybody else. The case is about military discipline, says the Court, not religion.

(And before anybody objects to my subsuming these decisions as part of the liberal constitutional project, claiming that
the Court that decided them in the mid-1980s was conservative, not liberal, bear in mind that my reference is to a hege-
monic vision of the nation as a single community with a single
set of values. It does not matter, for purposes of critique, which

contemporary political movement likes or dislikes those values; it matters only that the values are externally imposed through a process that does not treat the survival of communities and their traditions as a weighty variable.)

There have been moments—few and far between, but moments—when the project of liberal constitutionalism has carved out tiny spaces for the construction of dissenting communities of meaning that are able to exist free of some of the occasionally stultifying strictures of a civic order resting on the imposition of values in the guise of rights. Because I obviously favor the creation of spaces in which communities of meaning can thrive, one of my favorite Supreme Court decisions of the modern era—by which I mean the era after *Brown*—is *Wisconsin v. Yoder*,[31] decided in the early 1970s, and one of the decisions I find most troubling, even if in some sense inevitable, is *Board of Education of Kiryas Joel v. Grumet*,[32] decided in June of 1994.

Yoder granted to the Old Order Amish the privilege to violate the state's compulsory school attendance laws by removing Amish children from school after the eighth grade. The Amish way of life emphasizes a separation from the modern, and is born of the experience of their Anabaptist forebears, who suffered oppression and murder by a powerful and hostile external community. Without constitutional protection, the majority recognized in a mildly condescending opinion, the Amish way of life would cease to exist.

This much may seem obvious. But Justice William Douglas, in his dissent, fulminated against this approach for ignoring the rights of the children, thereby insisting on the privilege of the state to replace the Amish understanding of the world, which critics have attacked as totalizing, with what we might call rights-totalitarianism, an externally imposed vision of the only possible correct way to look at individuals as they stand in relationship to their communities. Defenders of *Yoder* point to the responsibility of the family as primary. Critics argue (correctly) that the family can make poor decisions. But by invoking the specter of the totalizing family as the ground for a different decision, the critics are assuming what the project of liberal constitutionalism invariably assumes: that the larger political sovereign will usually make better decisions than the family, or the community, will. Need I add that this presumption, too, is a cause of alienation of citizens from mainstream politics?

The second case that bears attention is *Board of Education of Kiryas Joel v. Grumet.* There, the Justices more or less dismantled the school district of the Village of Kiryas Joel, a small town about thirty-five miles north of New York City. The facts are in some ways similar to Yoder's and in some ways quite different, which is why I am not quite prepared to say that the case is wrong.

All the residents of Kiryas Joel are Satmar Hasidim, and nearly all the children of the community attend parochial schools. The village operated only a single public school, which served the needs of disabled students. The reason this situation came about was simple: the parochial schools were unable to provide for the special needs of the disabled. For a time, the villagers sent those children to a nearby public school that was better equipped to serve them. But the experiment failed because the other children made fun of their garb, their traditions, and their accents, so the parents understandably withdrew them from the public school to spare them "the panic, fear and trauma" that they suffered. Next, the villagers petitioned the legislature for permission to form a school district of their own, which was granted. The new school district then established a single public school, where the children could learn in what their parents believed would be a more supportive atmosphere.

But according to the Supreme Court, the very existence of the Kiryas Joel school district was a special favor the legislature had bestowed upon a religious group. The evidence was in the village's demographics: everybody in the town is of the same religion, so a political favor to the town is a political favor to a religion. "The fundamental source of constitutional concern here," wrote Justice Souter for the majority, "is that the legislature itself may fail to exercise governmental authority in a religiously neutral way." In other words, special treatment (as the Court described it) for the Satmar community might grant one religious group a special privilege that others, religious and non-religious, were denied.

The *Kiryas Joel* opinion is troubling because of this strange notion that the special accommodation for the Satmar constituted a threat to the religious freedom of others. Quite aside from the fact that once one moves beyond our urban areas, the nation is full of religiously homogeneous public school districts in which, presumably, children do not make fun of the accents or traditions or clothing of other children, it is difficult to imagine that the Satmar Hasidim really are the special favorites of the law. After the Court agreed to hear the case, one commentator noted, with heavy sarcasm, that the Justices had foiled New York's secret plot "to establish Hasidim Judaism as the official religion."

Community, Tradition, and Education

The reason that *Kiryas Joel* and *Yoder* are such important signposts is that a religious community's efforts to transmit its understandings of the world over time—to ensure the survival of its narrative—will often be most vital, and also most at risk, in the education of the community's children. This is why the Supreme Court decision most supportive of the survival of religious communities is almost certainly *Pierce v. Society of Sisters*,[33] in which the Justices struck down a state law requiring all students to attend public schools, a law that made the operation of private religious schools impossible, and was clearly intended to do so. The Court rested its decision on a principle that is, nowadays, all too often ignored: "the liberty of parents and guardians to direct the upbringing and education of children under their control."

Religious schools are a crucial tool in the ability of the religious communities to preserve their narratives over the generations. Nowadays, the principal constitutional battle on religious education is over the issue of whether state funds (what we like to call "tax dollars," although in these days of deficits it is difficult to tell) can be used to support them. Most scholars say *no* and the Supreme Court stands squarely on both sides of the issue—the state, for example, may supply religious schools with textbooks but not with maps.[34] My own view is simpler: protecting the freedom of religion means nurturing the ability of the religious communities to survive, which means, at a minimum, not treating religious entities worse than non-religious entities. Thus, if the state makes aid of any sort available to *any* private schools, it cannot refuse to make that aid available to those schools that happen to be religious. This non-discrimination principle applies independent of whether you happen to think that state aid to private schools is a good idea. (Certainly the state has no *obligation* of financial support to *any* private schools.) But if aid to private schools is offered, I do not see how any coherent vision of religious freedom can hold that religious schools are to be excluded from the recipients.

I emphasize this point because I worry that our contemporary debates about religious education, whether aided or unaided by state dollars, are carried on in substantial ignorance of history. This is not the place to recapitulate the story of the uneasy two-century relationship between religion and public education in the United States; that has already been done in many places, most recently in an excellent (if occasionally polemical) book by the historian Warren A. Nord.[35] I do think it worthwhile, however, to dip into a corner of that history in order to explain why religious schools have always been important to Americans who feel that their religious beliefs mark them as outsiders, which in turn should aid us as we struggle to find ways to ensure that religious communities are able to preserve their traditions across the generations.

Our tradition of religious freedom is precisely what makes the public schools problematic, both in theory and in history. As many observers have noted, religion is the only sphere that the Founders singled out for special constitutional protection against all forms of government intrusion. Much as we may, with good reason, cherish the right to privacy, for example, we must admit in our sober hours that it is not mentioned in the Constitution and that the effort to put it there and keep it there has required a willed suspension of disbelief among judges, lawyers, and scholars. And although some freedoms are spelled out with care—speech and the press, fortunately, are prominent among them—only religion carries with it the additional promise of the Establishment Clause. "Congress shall make no law respecting an establishment of religion," the First Amendment begins. We can have official government speech and official government publication. We cannot have an official government religion. This special solicitude toward religion has served the nation well, not only because, as I have mentioned, it provides us with ready-made sources of dissent, but, more important, because it provides a sphere in which one is free to contemplate the ultimate without external interference of any kind—a spiritual need that, left unfulfilled, often leaves a gaping hole in the soul.

America has long been aware of the ways in which this attitude of openness toward religion marks us as distinct among nations. Alexander Hamilton, while serving as Secretary of the

Treasury in 1791, wrote that immigrants would be attracted to the United States in part because we offered something "far more precious than mere religious toleration"—namely, "a perfect equality of religious privileges."[36] History has proved Hamilton partly right—the immigrants came, and continue to come, in huge numbers.

But history has also proved him partly wrong, and this is the point of my story. By the middle years of the nineteenth century, American resentment of immigrants had blossomed, and a principal focus of that resentment was the anti-Catholicism that quickly came to be summed up in a two-word slogan: "No Popery."[37] Indeed, anti-Catholicism was rampant even when Hamilton was writing. Some historians have argued that French Canadians did not join the American Revolution precisely because, as a predominantly Roman Catholic community, they felt a greater freedom to worship under English rule than what they sensed might flow from the anti-Catholic bigotry in the colonies. And, as William Lee Miller has persuasively shown, many of the strongest supporters of religious liberty, including some of the drafters of the First Amendment, chose the word "liberty" to describe their ideal precisely because they hoped that it would be understood to exclude those they dismissed as "mass sayers."[38]

This original "Native-American" movement, as it was ironically called by the grandchildren of immigrants who founded it, had some mild political successes, eventually even electing a handful of congressmen. But it took the nation by storm in the 1850s after its evolution into the Know-Nothing Order, a secret society working for political power and requiring its members to swear "that you will not vote or give your influence for any man for any office . . . unless he be an American-born citizen, in favor of Americans ruling America, nor if he be a Roman Catholic."[39] The Know-Nothings readily acknowledged their own nature as a secret society, and admitted that such societies are dangerous. But the secrecy was necessary, one Know-Nothing essayist argued, to combat the Roman Catholic Church, "a secret society" that was "absolutely controlled by its priesthood to a degree which has never been exercised by the leaders of any political party in this or any other country."[40]

The Know-Nothings were anything but a fringe. In the 1854 election, the party won the state of Massachusetts, electing a governor and controlling both houses of the legislature.[41] It had similar success in Delaware. There and elsewhere, the Know-Nothings painted themselves as the true Republicans, more pure than the national party, in which immigrants were said to be gaining influence, and certainly superior in virtue to the Southern Democrats. But everywhere, the Know-Nothings painted themselves as the protectors of America against the onslaught of what they called "Romanism." As one Know-Nothing essayist put it: "We regard the Pope as an imposter; and the Mother Church as the mother of abominations."[42]

Ironically, the Know-Nothings were finally destroyed, as the Union itself so nearly was, over the issue of slavery. The party's southern chapters were perhaps the more consistent: they despised Catholics, Jews, slaves, immigrants, nearly everybody, or so it seemed. The party chapters in the free states were more complex. They may have hated Roman Catholics, but, in one of those peculiar paradoxes of American politics, they were for freeing the slaves, by war if necessary. Indeed, they believed that the southerners had conspired to allow Catholics and other immigrants into the United States in large numbers in order to obtain their votes,[43] a variation on a popular nineteenth-century fantasy called "slave power," under which the slaves were the weapons with which the South would ultimately sink the North.

The Know-Nothing era, of course, was only the most open and unapologetic episode of anti-Catholicism in our history. There have been many other powerful anti-Catholic organizations, from the American Protective Association to the Ku Klux Klan, and even, in its early days, the National Education Association. There were frequent religious riots. In San Francisco and Louisville, Catholics were hanged. In Philadelphia and Baltimore (where American Catholicism began), they were shot in the street. During the late nineteenth and early twentieth centuries, anti-Catholic tracts were frequent bestsellers, and the estimable Justice William Douglas unashamedly cited one of the worst of them in an opinion as late as 1971.[44]

I recite this unhappy and often unremarked history to make a larger point about the public schools. Given what we know of their history, and their role in the attempted destruction of religious traditions, it is astonishing to hear us still arguing now, in the late twentieth century, about whether religious schools deserve public funds. In almost any other area of national life that had the same history, we would be debating the justice of the institution itself. Put otherwise, why do we assume that public schools are the norm and religious schools the aberrant intruder? I could well imagine a religious parent who understands the history looking at matters quite the other way around.

Let's go back again to the nineteenth century. William Seward, during his twenty years as governor of New York, argued that the immigrant children should have their own schools, perhaps paid for by public funds, because anti-Catholic prejudices made it impossible for them to attend the public schools. When he referred to impossibility, he did not mean official segregation—the laws did not ban the attendance of Catholics and Jews. But parents, Seward argued, often kept their children home rather than send them to learn at places where their religious traditions would be held up to ridicule. If you detect echoes of Seward's argument in the concerns of the Hasidic parents of Kiryas Joel, you are absolutely right.

And just as in the 1990s, the ridicule of which Seward spoke was real. Some of it was religious. For example, Catholic children, when reading required devotions during the school day, were required in many places to use Protestant Bibles. In May of 1844, Protestants rioted in Philadelphia, burning houses and churches and killing a number of people, all because of *rumors* (which turned out to be false) that the Catholics were trying to get the Bible out of the public schools. Two months later there was a second riot, after rumors spread that the city's Catholics were arming themselves. These rumors turned out to be true— and who could blame them?

Now this might lead you to conclude that the real problem was the devotional Bible readings. Were the public schools not in the business of trying to teach religion, one might argue, there would have been no crisis. But this analysis supposes, wrongly, that the only pedagogical threat to the survival of a religion is the teaching of another religion. There are other threats. The school may, and probably should, set itself the project of turning children into good citizens. The trouble arises when the school's vision of good citizenship is different from the vision held by the parents. And do not rush, at this crucial juncture, into the trap of liberal constitutionalism, and assume that the parents who have objections will be backward and malevolent, whereas the schools that teach their children what the parents do not want them to learn will be progressive and beneficent. Just consider a bit more of the history.

From the earliest times, public education in America has been understood, first and foremost, as training for citizenship. The nation's schools were to be the repository of the nation's values. The great exponent of the schools Horace Mann made the connection clear in an early-nineteenth-century essay defending compulsory public education:

> In a republican government, legislators are a mirror reflecting the moral countenance of their constituents. And hence it is, that the establishment of a republican government, without well-appointed and efficient means for the universal education of the people, is the most rash and foolhardy experiment ever tried by man . . . It may be an easy thing to make a republic; but it is a very laborious thing to make Republicans . . .[45]

In the early twentieth century, as the public schools began to take more solid hold, these sentiments were repeated and even expanded by the supporters of public education, the estimable John Dewey very much to the fore.[46] If we were not, yet, one people, they argued, why, then, universal schooling would make us so.

Now in a sense, all of this is unexceptionable. Democracy is a disaster if the citizens are morally obtuse. Moral training must come from somewhere. Mann, Dewey, and others argued that government must do its part, and that the way for government to do it was to organize schools and compel all children to attend. Otherwise, we would face a nation of moral illiterates.

Even today, the rhetoric rings true. We like to pretend that we have invented something called "value-free education," but we also know that to be a convenient myth. Education, by its nature, does indeed inculcate values, and the schools play their role. The question we face today, as the "character education" movement gathers steam, is whether to continue to teach values in the haphazard manner that is unavoidable when there is no plan, or to try to be deliberate about it.

Many religious parents object to the teaching of values—even common values—in the public schools, arguing with some force that an account of what matters without any hint of why it matters is pointless, perhaps self-defeating. Most parents evidently believe that the ultimate measure of moral truth is the will of God, and the public schools surely cannot teach that. Remember, however, our metaphor of the three-legged stool: moral knowledge is taught in the home, the school, and the place of worship, or it is not taught at all. If the schools are reinforcing the moral lessons the children learn at home and at church or synagogue, there will be little need for the schoolteachers to explain where the values come from; on the other hand, if the home and the place of worship do not do their jobs, we can hardly expect the schools to do it alone.

Of course, if we are explicit about teaching values, about telling children the difference between right and wrong, we run the marvelous psychological risk that we may actually have to *talk* about right and wrong, to discuss morality in order to discover what we hold in common. We adults, in other words, will be required to engage in public moral dialogue as we search together for this American core. And if we are reluctant to do so—if we refuse to see our public schools as places where values are to be taught—then there are two shattering consequences.

First, if we pretend that we can educate our children with no attention to morality, then we undercut the egalitarian ambitions of the public school movement. The schools become instead a tool of modern capitalism, a place where children learn the skills that will enable them to be productive workers—or, as we like to say as we camouflage that reality, to earn a living. Certainly every parent wants his or her children to learn a skill. But few parents consider what amounts to vocational training as the only reason to send their children to a school over which the parents have little control.

This leads to the second problem. If the public schools are not a good place to teach a set of values that we might think of as the American core, then there are no plausible defenses against the demands of parents for school voucher programs allowing tax dollars to be spent on private schools. A majority of parents say that they would send their children to private religious schools if they could afford to, and the number one reason they offer is that they want the schools to reinforce the values the parents are trying to teach them. In principle, there is no reason that the public schools cannot do the same thing. And if the schools refuse to do so, then parents will have a point when they argue that the schools are trying—actively trying—to wean their children from the religious traditions of the parents.

The trouble is, even if a school does try to teach this set of core values, it may sometimes make matters worse. John Dewey, this century's great apostle of public schooling, quite famously saw the public schools as places where the immigrant children would be "Americanized" or "democratized"; but the immigrant parents, when they saw what the schools were actually engaged in, believed that what was really going on was that Catholic and Jewish children were to be "Protestantized." So the parents did what Seward (and, in an earlier incarnation, Dewey) had suggested: they established their own schools, where the religious traditions that had nurtured them could be nurtured in turn.

And they were wise to do so, because there is good reason to think that the plan was just as the parents feared. Even in the early days of what were then called the common schools, as one historian has noted, the dominant values taught in the schools "were to be, unsurprisingly, the dominant values of the American culture and the growing middle class: Protestantism, capitalism, and Americanism."[47] One study of textbooks concluded that the aim of the public schools by the turn of the century was to replace the love of what was viewed as a foreign God with a love of America as a country[48]—very much the Know-Nothing program, long after the party itself vanished from the scene. Indeed, the program of public schooling itself began as a government response to the Protestant ideal, and was defended during the nineteenth century in explicitly religious terms.[49] The Catholic tradition, by contrast, had long located responsibility for education of the young in the family and the church[50]—which is precisely what the Protestants were afraid of. The law against sectarian education that Oregon adopted at the turn of the century and that the Supreme Court ultimately struck down in *Pierce* flowed from precisely this sentiment: the goal was quite plainly to destroy the power of the Catholic Church by ridding the nation of its Catholic schools. The prohibitions on state funding for religious education stem from the same era, and from the same reasoning: perhaps if these Romanist schools were denied money, they would collapse.[51]

Dewey himself, a follower of the trendy anti-religious psychology of his day, argued against formal religious instruction for the young because children should not be "inoculat[ed] externally with beliefs . . . which adults happen to have found serviceable to themselves." Religious education, wrote Dewey at a time when several states were trying to forbid it, was simply a form of segregation.[52] Far better, it seems, to get all the children into the public schools, where we would have the chance to shake them free of their immigrant superstitions.

Contemporary Lessons

Now, you might object: That is all ancient history. Whatever was wrong with the schools then, we do it better now. The complaints are no longer valid.

Many parents, however, continue to believe that the complaints are valid. A majority of the parents of public school children say they would send their children to private schools if

45

they could afford it—a shocking statistic in a nation supposedly devoted to the primacy of family—and, of those, the overwhelming majority say they would choose a religious school. The reasons cited by parents today (when many and perhaps most of those complaining appear to be Protestants) are precisely those cited by the Catholic and Jewish parents a century ago: the schools, they believe, are trying to wean their children from the religious faith of their parents, an activity that the parents view, with reason, as actively hostile to the survival of their religious traditions.

One may reply to this argument in three different ways, and the reply that we choose will say much about the weight we place today on our reinterpreted Declaration of Independence notion that justice is ultimately measured by the dissent of the governed.

First, we may say to the parents what the Supreme Court has already said, in too many cases, in too many ways. We may say, "It does not matter if your religious tradition survives or not. We, the government, have important work to do, and if our work threatens your survival, then it is your survival that will have to be sacrificed." Which, being translated, means religious freedom does not apply to dissenters.

Second, we may say what many in the educational establishment have said, since Dewey and perhaps since Horace Mann: "We are in a far better position than you are to know what your children need in order to become good, productive citizens in the way that we, who are charged with such matters, define those terms. So stop complaining and get with the program." Which, being translated, means religious freedom does not apply to families.

Third, we may say what we too rarely say—what the Supreme Court remembered in *Yoder* and forgot in *Kiryas Joel*—and what the early John Dewey, who, like Seward, urged the immigrants to build separate schools, understood, and the later John Dewey, who launched the project of "Americanization," did not. "We respect your concerns," we might say. "We respect your efforts to preserve your religious tradition, even when we do not understand or even care for the tradition itself. We respect your choice to preserve that tradition through your children. And, holding only an exception for physical harm to the child, we are prepared to do what is necessary to assist you in the choice that you have made." Which, I hope, does not need to be translated.

To continue to make the first two choices, I suspect, will only reinforce the feelings of alienation that drive voters away from the political mainstream, that make them believe that they have named evil and it is government. If we continue to make the first two choices, moreover, we will be doing precisely what the Declaration of Independence teaches us we should not: we will be meeting "repeated Petitions" only with "repeated injury." And in so doing we will create fertile ground not only for the seeds of dissent, but, ultimately, for the seeds of disallegiance; for we will teach instead that our "free" society counts among the powers of government the power to use education as the lever to eradicate unwanted religious traditions.

Some Objections, Some Replies, and Some Transitions

Now, you might object to this analysis on a fairly obvious ground: isn't it possible that the parents will want the child to learn something that is reprehensible?

My answer is yes, of course that is possible—but I do not see it as an objection. After all, the sovereign that controls the public schools might also want the child to learn something that is reprehensible. Once we abandon the stereotype of the religious parent as some sort of closed-minded irrational automaton, there is no evident reason to suppose that the sovereign that controls the public schools is *less* likely than the family to make a curricular choice that is reprehensible.[53] Horror stories about what this or that religious parent allegedly did are something of a drug on the market—but so are horror stories about what this or that public school or teacher allegedly did. I recognize that the inherent bias of liberal constitutionalism simply *presumes* that the sovereign will make a better set of decisions than the parents will: this is the bias that underlies, for example, Justice Douglas's dissent in *Yoder*, which I mentioned before. But if it is bias that is driving our judgment about the relative likelihood of good decisions by the family and good decisions by the sovereign, I fear that I, at least, will wind up casting my lot with the family.

There is a deeper point here. It is not sufficient to engage in a utilitarian calculus. The freedom of the family to make religious choices—a freedom that is essential if religious communities are to be able to survive by projecting their narratives over time—must include the freedom to make choices other than the best. That is what freedom *is:* the privilege of making mistakes. It will not suffice to say that we do not allow parents to make mistakes where their children are concerned; if that is the case, given the statistics that we face, we should not allow a single parent to drive a car in which a child is present, for we kill thousands of children a year that way. If we allow parents to drive with children, we should certainly allow them to make educational choices, which, to my knowledge, kill nobody.

Or one might offer a different objection, harking back to Horace Mann and perhaps John Dewey, and observing that we must have as many children as possible in public schools because that is where we build our citizens by inculcating the values we might think of as the American core. As I noted earlier, that argument is actually quite a strong one, provided always that we can find consensus on a core so that we actually have something for the schools to inculcate. The key word here is "consensus." To see why, just imagine the plight of the dissenting religious parent who does not happen to like the values that the public schools are teaching—again, the situation of so many Jewish and Catholic parents one hundred years ago. If you say to that parent, "Your child must learn these values because an elite group that is not answerable to your concerns has decreed it," you have not even made an argument worth answering. If you say instead, "Your child must learn these values because a majority of your fellow citizens have decreed it," the parent may not like the values, and the parent may even keep the child home, but at least you will have invited the parent to join a dialogue, thus showing the respect for the fellow citizen that successful democracy requires; more important, you will have made the argument from democracy, an argument that every citizen of the republic is bound to respect.

Perhaps this is an appropriate place to stop. I have talked today about the ways in which our concepts of allegiance sometimes interfere with the efforts of religious communities to maintain their narratives across the generations. I have proposed that we treat those concerns with the utmost respect, especially in the crucial area of education, where it does seem to me that ultimate authority should be ceded to the family. Only in this way, I have argued, can we avoid transforming the current mood of alienation into a popular sentiment of disallegiance like the sentiment reflected in the Declaration of Independence.

In the second lecture, I will consider a second aspect of the problem of dissent: what we do when the struggles for meaning in these communities conclude with decisions not just to believe, but to act; and to act in ways that violate secular law. The problem is one that we often believe we have resolved through some set of legal rules or other; but in our violent, unsettled culture, as I hope to show, we have actually settled almost nothing at all.

2

Disobedience

IN THE FIRST LECTURE, I argued that if we reinterpret the Declaration of Independence as an argument about dissent rather than consent, we discover that the justice of the sovereign turns in large measure on how it answers the complaints—what Jefferson called the "repeated Petitions"—of those who are subject to its authority. I suggested that in contemporary America, which so often seems riven by division and alienation, we must tread with care when facing dissent. I argued against the project of liberal constitutionalism, the effort to knit the nation into a single community sharing a single normative vision of the world, and, in particular, argued for the importance of nurturing the ability of our many religious communities to project their perhaps quite different normative understandings across the generations—a task that might require close community control of the education of their children.

In this second lecture, I will meditate on a variation on the same theme. Granting that America is a better nation and a far more democratic one if it provides a civic atmosphere in which the religions can survive and even thrive, there will naturally come times when the will of the secular sovereign will come into conflict with the very different moral understanding of the self-constituted communities of faith that it has nurtured. If the religious community refuses to knuckle under, the political sovereign will immediately define the inconsistency as disobedience of law—the same way, as it happens, that the religious community might define the actions of any of its members who should follow the competing will of the political sovereign.

These conflicts, as I will explain, do little to illuminate the practical or theoretical complexities of modern doctrines of civil disobedience. They do illustrate, however, a key point from the first lecture: the tendency of even a liberal political sovereign to become totalizing and the related reluctance of the law to acknowledge the possibility that people's lives will be richer and, literally, more meaning-full if they are able, as often as possible, to treat their religious traditions with all the same respect and presumptive obedience that is commanded by their allegiance to the secular political sovereign. I do not argue that in a contest of wills, the religious side must always win. I do believe that there is a scary, totalitarian aspect to the suggestion that it should usually lose. And I must warn today as I warned yesterday: if we deny religious people those possibilities, we are not merely being anti-democratic and ignoring the promise of our own Declaration of Independence; we are also fertilizing the ground of disaffection and, ultimately, of disallegiance. If on the other hand we are to grant these possibilities, there remains for the third lecture the question of just how we are to do it.

Disobedience and Definition

Whenever a community constitutes itself, it engages in an act of self-definition. If the community defines itself according to moral norms or epistemological premises different from those of the larger political community within which it dwells, it is already engaging in an act of disobedience. In liberal theory, even if the sovereign is indifferent among competing comprehensive visions of the good, it nevertheless creates and enforces a set of background rules against which those who would pursue their own visions must operate. The community that defines itself is potentially a threat as soon as it moves to constitute itself according to a different set of rules.

This point matters more in the liberal state (and thus in contemporary America) than it would in the "nightwatchman" state once beloved of libertarian theory. But the nightwatchman state has always struck those of us whom history has tended to oppress as a bit of a nightwatchmare, and I must say that despite the obviously devolutionist cast of the first lecture, I am overjoyed not to be living in one. I do believe in the need for background rules, and I do not believe that avoiding direct physical injury to the persons or property of others is enough.

Having said that, however, I must hasten to remind that one of the theoretical difficulties of the modern American state is the irritating insistence in our practical politics that *all* the rules are background rules, that every conclusion about right and wrong is one that the political sovereign—most notably, the *national* sovereign—should enforce through legislation on as many communities as possible. Left and right in America nowadays divide principally over the question of which conclusions to enforce, not over whether the national sovereign should be doing it. One sees this perhaps most obviously in the current debate over what is described, with some loss of coherence, as "welfare reform," a strange battle in which liberals try to command the states that there are certain people to whom they *must* give benefits and conservatives try to command the states that there are certain people to whom they *must not.*

For all the reasons set forth in the first lecture, my concern here is not with the "rights" of the states. On the contrary, I am troubled by our recent emphasis on federalism, with its celebration of unwilled and arbitrary geographic divisions, which I have labeled "geographic essentialism." Geographic essentialism is politically naive, constitutionally undesirable, and theoretically irrelevant. My concern is with the survival—here the word *right* would only mislead—of self-constituted communities of meaning, which suffer grievously when rhetorical tools developed for the purpose of criticizing the background rules of the national sovereign are presumed to be readily adapted to critique of the community. (This is simply the mirror image of the point of today's philosophers of liberalism, which boils down to a claim that the tools appropriate for critique within a religious community are not appropriate for a critique of the secular sovereign.)

The simplest example of the point is the criticism of those religious traditions that do not ordain women to the priesthood. Too often, the lay outsider will look at the religious community in question and complain that it does not allow women to exercise any "authority." This might be correct if one is in possession of a definition of authority that is easily translatable to communities that work from a different set of epistemological premises. But one cannot assume an easy translation. In most Christian communities, for example, the designated function of the clergy is service, not the exercise of authority. The vision of a pastor as issuing edicts to a congregation of automatons is simply an antireligious stereotype; in the particular, and well-documented, case of American religion, the faithful tend to be sternly resistant to the notion of hierarchical command.[1] Indeed, even the religious figure most often cited as exercising immense spiritual authority, the Pontiff of the Roman Catholic Church, must answer to God for his stewardship of the souls of a billion Roman Catholics. Of course, one who does not believe in God will not find anything interesting in this argument, but that simply makes my epistemological point—for the outsider to insist on his or her own vision of what constitutes the exercise of "authority" is to deny the ability of the community to constitute itself according to its own meanings.[2]

The nation has a long and unhealthy tradition of using its laws of general application to try to remake self-constituted communities of meaning in the model preferred by a larger culture. The delicate historical minuet between religious communities and objectionable rules of the secular political sovereign has been well-canvassed elsewhere,[3] but nevertheless deserves brief discussion here.

Consider: no question is as important to human existence as whether God exists, so, naturally, philosophy ignores it. Law, however, answers it, and the answer the law gives is often No. Take the famous case of *Reynolds v. United States* (1879),[4] in which the Mormons discovered that their constitutional right to freedom of religion did not extend to the practice of polygamy—in short, that they were not free, within the confines even of their own places of worship, to marry whomsoever they might choose. (The statute also took away the church's property and even its incorporation.) A lineal descendant of *Reynolds*, decided a bit more than a century later, is *Employment Division v. Smith* (1990),[5] in which adherents of the Native American Church discovered that their constitutional right to freedom of religion did not extend to the use of peyote—in short, that they were not free, within the confines even of their own places of worship, to ingest whatsoever they might choose. The cases (there are literally scores of others) allow the state to put the members of the religious communities in question to a simple choice: follow the law or follow your God. Because the First Amendment expressly protects religious freedom, it is difficult to defend the judicial permission for this choice except on an argument that runs something like this: it doesn't matter if the secular sovereign makes it difficult for you to practice your religion, because there are lots of other religions out there, and you can choose one of the others instead.

I emphasize the point because the reasoning in these cases may have theological as well as philosophical roots. The cases are linked by the nation's continuing fealty in its public law to a high-church Protestant vision of the distinction between belief and action—a distinction that is fairly easy to draw in a society so dominated by high-church Protestant values that it rarely forces adherents of mainline Protestant denominations to make a choice between the two.* (Even when it does, it doesn't. High-church Protestants avoided their own *Smith* case during Prohibition, when the Volstead Act, forced on them by their low-church brethren, made an explicit exception for the religious use of wine, which most high-church Protestants indulge and most low-church Protestants do not.) In this common and quite narrow version of the belief/action distinction, religionists are free to believe whatever they like, but have no rights to do anything in particular to follow their beliefs. The justification for this distinction as a rule of constitutional law was stated by Justice Antonin Scalia in his majority opinion in *Smith:*

> It may fairly be said that leaving accommodation to the political process will place at a relative disadvantage those religious practices that are not widely engaged in; but that unavoidable consequence of democratic government must be preferred to a system in which each conscience is a law unto itself or in which judges weight the social importance of all laws against the centrality of all religious beliefs.[6]

So if a religious belief happens to require a violation of secular law, the disobedient religionist who follows that belief loses.

Sometimes—rarely—religionists who want to turn their acts of dissenting belief into acts of dissenting conduct slip through

---

*My use of the terms "high-church Protestant" and "low-church Protestant" is not meant to imply any judgments on the relative merits of Protestant denominations. It is consistent with the traditional usage in the sociology of religion, although some scholars have come to prefer "high-status Protestant" and "low-status Protestant." (The high-church or high-status Protestants tend to be organized hierarchically and to follow in important respects the Anglican or other European Protestant traditions, and include, among others, Episcopalians, Lutherans, and Presbyterians. The low-church or low-status Protestants tend to have their origins in the dissenting church movements and include, among others, the Baptists and the Pentecostals.)

this rather widely cast net. In a few notable cases, as in the conscientious objector exceptions to the Selective Service laws, the possibility is granted by statute. And on very rare and special occasions, the possibility is granted by a court. In the first lecture, I lauded the Supreme Court's 1972 decision in *Wisconsin v. Yoder*,[7] allowing families of the Old Order Amish to remove their children from the public schools after the eighth grade, a judgment the Justices placed on the ground that further formal education was unnecessary to the Amish way of life and would indeed make that way of life more difficult to sustain. I defended the decision against secular critics who argue that it ignored the "rights" of children, insisting instead on a constitutional space within which communities that define themselves as constituted of believing families rather than atomistic individuals are able to function.

As I mentioned at the outset, however, victories by religious freedom plaintiffs in cases of this kind are relatively infrequent. The Religious Freedom Restoration Act, enacted by the Congress in 1993 and signed into law by President Clinton, might eventually have made a difference in the ratio of wins to losses, but the Supreme Court declared it unconstitutional in 1997 (after these lectures were delivered).[8] Even before the Court acted, there were reasons to doubt that the Act really made a large difference.[9] Nevertheless, one must admit that the oppressive version of the belief/action distinction that the Supreme Court has lately followed in religious freedom cases was at least openly challenged by the statute's requirement that a law working a significant infringement on the exercise of religion be sustained by a showing that enforcement of the law is necessary to serve a compelling state interest.

But the belief/action distinction is likely to survive, both in our jurisprudence and, more important, in our philosophical and political rhetoric, and that survival is possessed of a political dimension. It is a genuine curiosity how a dominant liberal ethos that sometimes seemed to deny the belief/action distinction in the sixties and seventies, when the civilly disobedient tended to be protesting segregation or the Vietnam War, came to celebrate it in the eighties and nineties when the civilly disobedient tended to be protesting abortion. Unless one is prepared to argue that it is morally impermissible to hold the opinion that killing a fetus is a great moral wrong (the view, as it happens, of many millions of perfectly sensible American citizens), it is not easy to see why the belief/action distinction should be put to this peculiar use. Perhaps the belief/action distinction is less a tenet of philosophy than a tenet of power: that is, those who control the apparatus of the secular sovereign will always insist upon it, and those who inhabit self-constituted communities that consider themselves outsiders will always deny it. One would then expect particular emphasis on the distinction as power is concentrated in a single sovereign and the battles for control of that single sovereign grow increasingly bitter. Political science teaches that battles over the apparatus of state power are more bitter when more is at stake.

A particularly instructive instance of this tenet is the use of the power of the secular sovereign, both judicial and legislative, to remove pro-life protesters from defined zones in front of clinics where abortions are performed. It is, of course, vital to the notion of witness that the witnesses can be seen and heard; if they are moved, say, across the street from the entrance to a clinic, the witness itself becomes less effective. Proponents of special rules to keep the protesters away argue that in the absence of the rules, the practical effect of the protests will be to make women less likely to seek abortions. That this is the very point of the protests is a side issue. What is fascinating is the philosophy underlying the argument. If indeed First Amendment activity can be readily curbed when it interferes with the normal operation of whatever is being protested, one looks forward with some eagerness to national legislation banning protesters from shouting too loudly outside meetings or lectures on subjects they dislike. (The lecturer and the listeners have constitutional rights too.) That no such legislation is on the horizon suggests that my analysis is correct.

That is not to say that the belief/action distinction should be obliterated or that all activism in a particular cause is justified. After all (as we shall see) there may be lines beyond which it is not proper for the dissenter to travel. So the simple fact that the open dissent of self-constituted communities is both useful to our democracy and important to community survival does not address the quite distinct question of what tactics are appropriate. Indeed, one of the most troubling signs of our times is the growing willingness of the dissenters to be violent and even murderous in expressing their disagreements, a point to which I will turn after a brief interlude.

Disobedience and Community

The concept of civil disobedience, which is understood, if not fully accepted, in virtually every strand of liberal philosophy, rests on the moral obligation to resist injustice: even laws, if they are unjust, must be resisted. The idea that a law can be unjust is founded in the separation of law and morality without which no critical standpoint exists. In America, this separation, and the disobedience it implies, has a long and controversial tenure, and is by no means limited to the religious disobedients I have been discussing. My concern is not with religion as such but with religion as an example of a self-constituted community of meaning that may serve as a forum for seeking different understandings and, ultimately, as a focus for dissent.

In our nation's history, the shining exemplar of civil disobedience is of course the Reverend Martin Luther King Jr., whose leadership of a movement that practiced dissent through self-sacrifice is already the stuff of legend. His "Letter from Birmingham City Jail" is a classic document, for the study not just of civil disobedience but of American history itself. In the "Letter," King declared that the disobedient individual who breaks an unjust law as a form of protest and then "willingly accepts the penalty by staying in jail to arouse the conscience of the community" is "in reality expressing the very highest respect for law."[10]

This famous quote is hardly noncontroversial; on the contrary, the philosophy literature is full of disagreement on when and whether the disobedient has the obligation to stand punishment for breaking the law. Resolving that controversy is not my intention in the present lecture, although I will have something more to say about it in the third lecture. Rather, I want to emphasize a particular aspect of King's dissent, and of the official response to it: King's dissent was an act, not just a declaration of words, and it was for that act that he was punished. And what is particularly significant about the act is that it was an act not of a single individual but of an organized group.

America's legally constituted sovereigns have generally been less kind to dissenting groups than to dissenting individuals, perhaps because the one is more dangerous than the other. Indeed, this concern surely lies at the heart of the speech/action distinction that is so cherished in First Amendment theory. The freedom of speech, as the courts like to say, protects words, not actions, with the exception of a small set of actions that are, according to the judges, "communicative" in nature—flag burning being perhaps the most notorious example.[11] Because of the speech/action distinction, critics argue that the freedom of speech is useless to those who seek radical change.

Consider, for example, the case of Benjamin Gitlow, accused in 1920 of violating New York's Criminal Anarchy Act by preaching communism. Although defended by the estimable Clarence Darrow—who argued to the jury that Gitlow's writing was too "tame" and "dull" to have any effect—Gitlow was convicted. The Supreme Court, in a well-known opinion of which I will say more in the third lecture, sustained the conviction.[12] But I want to say a word here about the reasoning of the New York Court of Appeals (the state's highest court), which also sustained the conviction before the case ever reached the Supreme Court.

In the New York Court of Appeals, a majority voted to uphold the conviction, but two judges—Cuthbert W. Pound and Benjamin Cardozo (who would shortly be joining the Supreme Court) dissented. They argued that the First Amendment protected absolutely Gitlow's *advocacy* of "a change in our form of government" to what Pound called "Left Wing socialism." But the state would be perfectly free, the dissenters went on, to prohibit anyone from actually trying to change it. This move, made in many a First Amendment case over the years, reduces advocacy to hopelessness; the rule becomes, Preach whatever you like, as long as you are unconvincing—or, in Darrow's terms, "dull" and "tame." But if you are preaching about something serious, and if you begin to persuade others to act, why, then the state may stop you.

And there lies the point: by protecting advocacy only until it moves people to act, the courts have drawn not simply a speech/action distinction, but an individual/group distinction. The lone critic is no danger, because he can do nothing alone. But the group, because it is better able to act, becomes a threat. That is why those in power have always sought legal means to thwart *organizations* that are preaching dissent, while leaving ineffective individuals largely alone. This allows us to proclaim a respect for free speech, leaving unspoken the corollary, that speech will be left free only as long as it is ineffective.

Consider the antiwar movement of the 1960s, much of which was nurtured in what might fairly be described as communities—not the intense, close-knit communities of meaning that the religions represent, but the relatively closed community of the campus, where young and excited minds, desperate for knowledge (if not for wisdom) interact with each other, with their professors, and with the great texts that one hopes they still encounter. Certainly the campuses were centers of antiwar activism; so were the many organizations spawned in this era of mass dissent, from the Yippies to the Peace and Freedom Party to the Students for a Democratic Society. And the secular sovereign did not sit idly by as these communities formed their dissenting visions; as one historian has pointed out, the administrations of Presidents Johnson and Nixon between them "prosecuted virtually every prominent antiwar leader."[13] Why? Because the antiwar advocacy was having an effect. For similar reasons, the Federal Bureau of Investigation targeted the many organizations of what the historian Clayborne Carson calls "the black freedom struggle"—but principally in the 1950s and 1960s, when their advocacy began to move millions, not in the 1930s and 1940s, when most Americans, black and white, seemed to assume that the existing social order was set in stone.

But, again, it would be quite a serious error to envision the effort to stifle dissent at the very moment it becomes effective as principally an inclination of the American right. The left, too, has its innings, and makes the most of them. Shifting lines of political power tend to create shifting degrees of respect for such constitutional rights as free speech, which of course are designed to transcend (and therefore to mediate) questions of allegiance. Indeed, the saddest of the many tragic aspects of today's hubris-laden efforts to regulate so-called hate speech is that they have caused some liberals, who back in the fifties and sixties virtually discovered the First Amendment in the face of a complacent, allegiance-seeking majority, to forget the value of what they found. Perhaps, though, this is balanced by the way that American conservatism, much of which forty years ago seemed to think free speech a communist plot to weaken the nation, has come to understand the centrality of the First Amendment as a tool for resisting the tendency of Americans with power to suppress those who do not show allegiance to the same vision of what America is or ought to be.

This is perhaps the principal glory of our First Amendment tradition: properly understood, it frustrates *everybody*—or at least everybody possessing the will to censor debate and the political power with which to do it. A truly democratic polity could not hope to exist without it. And yet one can imagine a community, without sovereign authority, and so constituted that free speech, as we understand it in a political/constitutional sense, is either irrelevant or actually dangerous. A religious tradition, for example, might require, as the price of belonging, an adherence to a particular form of words, or, more practically, an agreement to forgo a certain form of words. For example, the Supreme Court ruled in *Cohen v. California*,[14] inevitably but uncomfortably, that expletives are protected speech. But a religion need not hold that blasphemy is protected speech. The United States may not punish a protester for using in the public square the language of the locker room, but a church may certainly punish a communicant for taking the name of the Lord in vain.

I am not here referring to the Constitution. Obviously, there is no constitutional restriction on a religion's decisions on the discipline of its members. What I mean is that even within a liberal polity, for the epistemological reasons I mentioned before, there is no obvious standpoint from which to criticize a church for punishing its members; and if there were, that polity would be less liberal. To suppose otherwise—to suppose that every institution through which citizens organize their lives must fit the model that the sovereign prefers—is to destroy the intermediary institutions that make bearable the simple fact, as true in a democracy as anyplace else, that one is governed. And the destruction of those institutions not only increases alienation—it also decreases the possibilities of open dissent, dissent in the useful sense of trying to constitute community in a way quite different from what the majority of one's fellow citizens may prefer.

Consider two examples. In the 1950s, the Roman Catholic archbishop of New Orleans, Bishop Rummel, issued a threat to excommunicate members of the state legislature who voted in favor of a school segregation measure then awaiting action. In the 1980s, the Southern Baptist Convention voted to withdraw "fellowship" (the only available sanction) from any congregation that "affirmed" homosexuality. In each case, the church was out of step with the evolving moral understandings of the society—but reflecting the results of the latest opinion polls is not the job of religion. In my secular self, I think the archbishop was wise and the Southern Baptists were not. As one who respects religious communities, not simply in their freedom, but in their autonomy to reach radically different understandings of life, I fully support the rights of each.

But my subject in this second lecture is not the ability of the community to define itself in ways that the larger society may disapprove—that, I hope, is well settled—but the ability of the community to define itself in ways that the larger society disapproves so strongly that it makes them illegal. For it is here that the cherished speech/action distinction cuts most sharply *away* from the protection of dissent, and toward the repeated rejection of the "repeated Petitions" for redress that lie, as I argued in the first lecture, at the heart of the Declaration of Independence.

Race, Repeated Petitions, and Disobedience

First, let me move outside the realm of communities that self-define along religious lines, and consider for a moment an obvious example of a well-defined community that has for centuries found its "repeated Petitions" met, not only with "repeated injury" but with determined announcements that its desired course of conduct amounts to a violation of law. I refer to the African-American community.

Consider first the two centuries of slavery. What could the slaves not do that others could? Sell their labor, obviously. Move where they desired and, in many cases, marry whom they wanted. In most of the South, slaves could not give evidence in court, and, of course, could not own property, particularly real estate. Once the slave rebellions began, it became widely illegal to teach slaves to read and write and, in many states, to preach the Gospel to them. (Were the slaves to become fellow Christians, the already specious justifications for enslavement would evaporate.) The list goes on, but the point should be clear: to be enslaved in the United States of America was not, as it was in many parts of the world, simply a matter of lifelong indentured servitude, although that would be wicked enough. It was not simply existence on the bottom rung of a caste system. Rather, it was to face a complex and totalizing network of *legal* restrictions so constructed as to make it a crime to engage in what we have come to regard as the ordinary occupations of life.

The century of Jim Crow was quite similar. Again, the laws worked restrictions on the freedom to make choices in life: choices about education, health care, housing, profession, even leisure time. (Consider segregated parks and swimming pools.) Again, normal life was not possible, because to live a normal life was illegal. When ordinary life becomes illegal, ordinary people become lawbreakers. Surely the universal historical appeal of Rosa Parks (as compared to, say, the controversy over affirmative action) rests precisely on her ordinariness: an ordinary person trying to do an ordinary thing—take a bus ride—finds herself in trouble with the law and thereby sparks a movement. The symbol carries power, for even the most indifferent white American could suddenly understand a tiny part of the life of segregated black America, the inability to do the little things, the ordinary things, that white Americans take for granted.

But the spark comes from her dissent, her breaking of the law, and without the dissent, the disobedience, the lawbreaking of the civil rights movement, the nation would not have changed as fast as it has or as much as it has. (The truth that the nation has a very long distance yet to travel should not blind us to the truth that it has already traveled a very long way.) And the dissent itself, the disobedience through lawbreaking, probably became inevitable once—in the words of the Declaration—the black community's "repeated Petitions" were met with "repeated injury."

Now, I do not mean to treat as insignificant the legal arm of the civil rights movement. That, too, involved a series of "repeated Petitions." And if the repeated petitions of both the protest wing and the litigation wing had been much longer ignored, I do not think there is any question that an act of "disallegiance" by black America would have been justified. I say *disallegiance* rather than *disobedience* to emphasize the distinction between breaking the law—disobedience—and rejecting the sovereign's claim to sovereignty—disallegiance. Although there were certainly groups of black activists who questioned the legitimacy of the constituted sovereign, both the protest and litigation wings of the movement were at pains to remind anybody who would listen that the black community was loyal, and wanted only fair play.

Now, you might have noticed my use of the term "black community." Let me make clear that I do not claim—and I do not believe—that there exists an identifiable set of black "meanings," as there often is, for example, in a religious community; that is, I do not believe in the existence of such a thing as the "black point of view."[15] So I am not in that sense an essentialist, and I quiver whenever smart professors who should know better assert that there is a unique "black perspective" (which they, of course, are uniquely able to identify). But I do believe that there is a black community, a community less of shared experience than of shared history, and a community which, even if it lacks normative authority or interpretive identity, nevertheless asserts a tug on its members—the tug, however complex its definition and effects, that we call racial solidarity. I consider that solidarity, in general, a good thing, even though it sometimes has ill effects.

Why should this sound remotely peculiar to the liberal ear? Civil society relies for its continuation on a broad panoply of voluntary and involuntary relationships that might create community in the sense of a place where members may feel that a degree of allegiance is owed: religious tradition, family, friendship, neighborhood, profession. There is no plain reason to exclude ethnicity, not even the practical difficulty of definition. It is true that our unhappy history teaches that the use of race to identify a community will often be used to oppress. But that is a reason for caution, not for prohibition: after all, the same is obviously true of the use of religion. What is most important, no matter how the community is defined, is that the definition reflects love of those who are members rather than hatred of those who are not—the distinction, for example, between the American Muslim Mission, led by Wallace (Warithuddin) Muhammad, and the Nation of Islam, led by Louis Farrakhan. When the issue is race, the pull of solidarity can be particularly strong, so that no matter what one's other professional, family, or community ties, race always exerts a tug, a tug one may answer through a love of one's own identity that extends in a unique way to the group.[16]

But does this identification advance our understanding of the role of the community in providing the base for dissent, not in the sense of protest, but in the sense of actual disobedience? I think it might—and I think one place to look might be not politics as such, but the economic system. Quite a number of theorists have recently picked up on the old black nationalist argument that African Americans owe less allegiance to the structure of American law than white Americans do because of the ways in which that structure has been used as a tool of racial oppression. Years ago, Angela Davis used this approach to argue, cleverly but unpersuasively, that all black people convicted in the nation's criminal courts are political prisoners. More recently, the legal scholar Regina Austin has made this notion the centerpiece of a quite sophisticated, and quite plausible, defense of market exchanges within the black community without regard to the economic regulations that apply to everyone else.

During the 1950s and early 1960s, mainstream civil rights organizations struggled mightily to resist this view, and this for two related reasons. First, they were worried that their members might be painted as less than law-abiding. Bear in mind that as originally conceived, the project of integration rested on what must seem rather quaint in our era of essentialism, the notion that skin color is irrelevant. Second, they were concerned quite concretely about being labeled Communists—meaning that their members would be painted not simply as lawbreakers, but as active participants in a clandestine struggle to overthrow the national community.

The resistance to the rhetoric of separateness was obviously crucial to a movement designed to force the existing national community to expand. Nowadays, the anti-essentialist aspects of the integrationist ideal have largely vanished from the thinking of leading black intellectuals, which, as many critics have pointed out, has led to an uneasy and so far unresolved tension between a demand to belong, which implies a redefinition of the larger community, and a demand to be acknowledged as a distinct culture, which implies the construction of a separate community.

Professor Austin has tried to mediate this tension a bit—at least in the economic realm. Stripped to its essence, her argument is that black Americans, because of both past and present racial oppression, owe a lesser duty of allegiance to the nation's laws than others might. Her case must be distinguished with some force from Angela Davis's argument that black Americans, for the same reasons, owe the nation's laws *no* duty of allegiance. Austin's case would be insurmountably difficult if framed in terms of a "right" to disobey the law, but although she occasionally lapses into such rhetoric, I do not think she means it. I think she has in mind a vision of the African America as a more or less self-constituted community of meaning, with independent norms that may govern the decision whether to obey the commands of the secular sovereign; not a community with the right to do as it chooses, but a community in possession of another set of imperatives to which it must sometimes answer. This set of imperatives I have already identified as *solidarity*.

Austin's principal point, which she has made more than once, is at its most effective in a small essay in the *Yale Law Journal* on the subject of the informal economy.[17] There she in effect calls for the community to self-constitute along particular lines that will assist in the development of a spirit of entrepreneurship, to overcome what she sees as an "antibusiness" bias in the black community as presently constituted. As she points out, however, entry costs to the legal entrepreneur may be sufficiently high to prevent black firms from entering the market. Consequently, she proposes that members of the community may wish to engage in market exchanges (for example, illegal vending) that the society formally forbids. She does not mean selling illegal products, such as drugs; she means selling legal products and services in ways that are illegal.

The conservative economist Walter Williams has argued that it is often the cost of entry, rather than racism as such, that prevents black entrepreneurs from entering the market—and that the entry costs are often kept high by government regulators. His example is the requirement in New York City and several other places that a potential market entrant obtain one of the limited supply of medallions (a license traded in the market) in order to drive a taxi. Because the demand for medallions is so much greater than the supply (which the city artificially suppresses), the cost of a medallion is quite high, especially in comparison with the resources of the inner-city entrepreneur. Williams proposes scrapping such regulations; Austin, if I read her correctly, proposes ignoring them. And New York's significant fleet of so-called gypsy cabs is evidence that the market is already providing what Austin suggests.

Austin's is certainly a vision of community in the sense that I contend, and it even has implications for dissent, because Austin argues that "for some poor blacks, breaking the law is not only a way of life; it is the only way to survive."[18] One could hardly ask for a clearer statement of meaning developed by a community, and, indeed, the community's self-perception of survival is at issue in many of the cases involving competing loyalties to separate sovereigns. One thinks, for example, of the *Lyng* case, in which the Supreme Court gave the back of its hand to three Indian tribes whose religious traditions would, in the majority's own word, be "devastated" if the Forest Service allowed logging on their sacred land.[19] One can hardly imagine a greater injustice than the destruction of a small, politically powerless religion for the sake of short-term economic gain, but the Justices allowed it to happen.

Disobedience and Violence (I)

Very well: Now we come to the hard part of any discussion of organized resistance to constituted authority. I refer, of course, to violence.

The problem of resistance to unjust laws is inexorably linked with the problem of violence, no matter what cause one selects as the one worth examining. Racial injustice, for example, was the rallying cry not only of Martin Luther King Jr., the most heroic nonviolent civil disobedient in our history, but also of John Brown, whose armed raid on Harper's Ferry was deliberately violent and was punished with deliberate state violence. Most contemporary scholars of civil disobedience are at pains to insist that the disobedience must be nonviolent to be morally appropriate. But I wonder whether this is correct. We tend to describe violence (we usually use the word "force," although it is scarcely more pleasant) as the exclusive prerogative of the sovereign. We describe it that way because, since Hobbes, that has been our *definition* of the sovereign: the entity which, within a prescribed area, holds the exclusive prerogative of violent force.

Must we so quickly concede that Hobbes is right? Generations of revolutionaries think not. And, indeed, once we accept the analytically difficult claim that an individual may believe himself loyal to two sovereigns at once—one temporal, for example, and one religious—we can see the complexity of the problem. The person who serves two sovereigns might argue that either one of them holds the prerogative of violent force, albeit across variously defined areas. For the secular sovereign, the realm of force is geographic, defined by national borders. For the religious sovereign, the realm might be spiritual and moral, defined by the borders of that morality. Thus, one might argue that the morality of the violent disobedient who is following the will of his religious sovereign over a moral question should not be judged by standards significantly different from the morality of the violent enforcer of the will of the secular sovereign—for example, the police.

Having just derived this proposition, I must hasten to add that I am terrified by it, because it could be cited as authority for terrorism of all kinds, including, in the American experience, the murder of physicians who perform abortions. Consider this graceful but chilling and, one hopes, somewhat ironic comment by Martin Buber in his famous 1929 essay entitled "Dialogue": "I have not the possibility of judging Luther, who refused fellowship with Zwingli in Marburg, or Calvin[,] who furthered the death of Servetus. For Luther and Calvin believe that the Word of God has so descended among men that it can be clearly known and must therefore be exclusively advocated."[20] In short words, Buber is saying that the believer who knows he is right may not hesitate to kill for his beliefs—and that others lack the basis to criticize him.

If Buber is right, might we not say the same of John Salvi, convicted of two 1994 fatal shootings at a Brookline, Massachusetts, abortion clinic? After all, if a pro-life protester is persuaded by his religious understanding that fetuses are human, that abortion is murder, and that physicians who perform abortions are thus, literally, baby-killers, why (other than moral cowardice, a fear to face the judgment of the society) should he not kill the doctors? The argument is an old one: If I have a gun in my hand and I see an adult about to kill a child and I have no other way to prevent the murder, surely I am justified in point-ing my weapon and killing the adult. The fact that the society disagrees is (in Buber's terms) irrelevant if I am sure that God teaches otherwise. The fact that my coreligionists disagree may also be irrelevant, because I could be right, and they, wrong. Thus does Buber's argument justify religious terrorism.

Pro-life terrorists often cite as inspiration the violent dissent of John Brown and his followers: if violence is permissible to end the great evil of slavery, then why not to end the great evil of abortion? The easy answer is that John Brown was not justi-fied either, an answer that is made easy only by our moral smugness 130 years after slavery ended. But I will pass that answer because I do believe that violence was justified in the battle against slavery, or, more precisely, I believe that the gov-ernment that tolerated enslavement of human beings had for-feited its exclusive prerogative to use force. This does not mean that every use of force by one of that government's opponents is thus legitimate—one still must find an independent moral justification—but it does mean that use of force by the (illegiti-mate) government's opponents is not automatically *less* legiti-mate than use of force by the government itself. So (following Buber), we might conclude that as long as the disobedient is certain that the practice he wishes to stop is sufficiently evil, we must not criticize him for his violence, unless we also criticize the state for its violence.

But Buber is surely wrong, at least in the implications of his assertion—wrong if not in the Europe of the days of Christen-dom then certainly in the United States of the twentieth cen-tury. The individual who is loyal to the religious sovereign should be willing to forgo the use of violence in a political soci-ety he deems basically fair and just, a society in which respectful dialogue is possible. Rarely is it possible to reach a general judgment about the society on the basis of a single unjust law.

But this does not quite resolve the matter, because a set of laws will sometimes render a society unjust, that is, an illegitimate sovereign, in which case its claim to the exclusive right to use force disappears. This was true of Nazi Germany even prior to the Holocaust: the racial laws alone were sufficiently totalizing and oppressive that the sovereign was illegitimate in liberal terms. The same was true of the United States in the era of slavery and for the most ruthless parts of the era of Jim Crow. In either case, Nazi Germany or the American slaveocracy, the fundamentally unjust sovereign had yielded its exclusive right to use force, which means that the disobedient, even the religious disobedient, could use force, too.

What other answers are possible? It is no answer to say what, in the end, the secular liberal wants to say—that slavery is wicked and abortion is not—because not everybody believes that. (In some surveys, a majority of Americans say they think abortion is as bad as killing a child.) And it is hypocritical for the secular liberal to say that the opponent of abortion should take his cause to politics, because the secular liberal thinks abortion is a constitutional right and thus should be outside the realm of politics. (As it happens, I think abortion should be in politics, not out of it, but that is rather a moot point.) The best answer is not political or philosophical, but theological: that God hates violence, and that the killer by his conduct mocks the very pro-life ethic that he cites as inspiration. The late Joseph Cardinal Bernadin, who frequently addressed this point, was precisely right: the ethic of life must be a seamless web.

Of course, the secular liberal will find this answer inadequate, and so will the pro-life terrorist. After all, it is enough for the killer to say "I disagree with you about God"—and we spin down the path to violence. But it may be that the political answer sounds in practicalities rather than in moral legitimacy. The one fact that the secular liberal knows is that if the pro-life terrorist kills, the law will treat him as a murderer. The United States, quite famously, has no concept of political prisoner, and the recent discovery by the left of the old "Silent Majority" slogans of law and order means that the killer goes to prison. Force is itself an argument, and it is, in practical terms, usually decisive. In short, even if the terrorist is unconvinced of the *legitimacy* of the political sovereign's claim to exclusive right to use force, he knows that the sovereign is, as between the two of them, much the better armed.

The point is by no means trivial, and it helps illustrate the error of Buber's approach (and thus of Salvi's). The reason is quite basic. Even if it is true, as I believe it is, that the existence of multiple sovereignties makes a hierarchy of *moral* authority impossible to establish, this result, at a minimum, simply weakens the claim of *either* sovereign to the right to resort to the ultimate sanction, which is killing. Thus it is a gross moral wrong for a pro-life protester to kill a physician and it is also a gross moral wrong for the state to execute him for doing it.

Yet this argument seems inadequate, because it seems to equate as moral propositions the action of the disobedient who does murder and the action of the state in capital punishment. Perhaps this is a proper equation—certainly important parts of the Christian tradition would hold that it is—but at the same time, one must recognize a certain moral casualness in the comparison. Even when two killings are both wrong, they are not necessarily wrong for the same reasons or in the same degree.

Yet the philosophical problem, although sensitive, is hard to avoid, once we begin to question the basic Hobbesian assumption. We are then left with the proposition that every act of violence requires an *independent* moral justification; in other words, "I'm just enforcing the law" doesn't count. A police officer would instead have to say, "I am enforcing a morally just law." Were someone else to ask "Sez who?" it would be no answer for the officer to point to some other authority, such as the court or the legislature, because the disobedient might simply answer, "So what?"

Once we begin this game, the iterations might be endless. Thus it may be that we cling to our Hobbesian definition of sovereignty—the exclusive prerogative on violence—because other paths lead, not to a life, as Hobbes so famously put it, that is "solitary, poor, nasty, brutish, and short," not to anarchy or lawlessness, but to the unthinkable need to offer a fresh moral defense of every official action. We would possess, in other words, no foundation of legitimacy on which to build. And so we retreat to Hobbes, not because he is obviously right, but because we cannot think how to do anything else.

Separate Sovereigns?

But we need not, yet, despair. The fact that there are multiple sovereigns does not mean that each is sovereign over an identical sphere.[21] Consider once more by way of example the case of the disobedient John Fries, who raised an armed militia to wage violent battle against both the state of Pennsylvania and the ill-fated federal property tax that the Congress enacted in 1798. Returning to Hobbes, we can distinguish the violence of Fries from the violence of the armed soldiers who at last arrested him, on the following ground: with some carefully drawn exceptions for instances of resistance to armed oppression, the exercise of armed force is the special privilege of the secular *political* sovereign. If there are other sovereigns—religious, for example—they, too, might hold certain exclusive privileges that nobody else (especially not the state) may exercise. Indeed, the belief that the state may not interfere with the moral and theological instruction of the religious sovereign is the key to much of the objection to the public school curriculum that I discussed in the first lecture: just as the church may not offer violence, say the parents, the state may not offer an ethic that competes with family religion.

The implications of this possibility are also a little scary. Grant the political sovereign its exclusive right to violence—in turn, the political sovereign must grant to, say, the religions the exclusive right to moral instruction. Certainly this balance was at the heart of the Roman Catholic argument against compulsory public education in the late nineteenth and early twentieth centuries, and, as we saw in the first lecture, it echoes in the arguments for public school vouchers that one hears today. The private religious school, in this vision, exists precisely because of the sovereign authority of religion over the moral education of the young. For the state to offer competing instruction in a public school, and to tax non-users to do it, the argument might run, is, in principle, no different from the choice by a religious organization to stockpile weapons: it represents the impermissible crossing of a definitional boundary. When the boundaries are freely transgressed, the continued existence of the sovereign itself (which is defined by the boundaries) is threatened. This would explain why the federal government would attack the Branch Davidian compound in Waco, but it would also explain why Christian Coalition and Excellence in Education would succeed in altering the content of school curricula and the membership of school boards.

Of course, the notion that each sovereign holds sway over its own sphere might seem to leave us back where we started, as morally casual as the original Hobbesian assumption, because, no matter how it is spruced up, it seems, at bottom, to assume the primacy of the will of the secular political sovereign over the will of any competing sovereign. That is the move that leads in the end toward a community-destroying statism of the sort that I condemned in the first lecture. I would like to think that we avoid this result, in part, through making the competing sovereigns real rather than metaphorical. For example, as I just suggested, we might decide that the state may never interfere with the religious sovereign's jurisdiction over the family, unless the religious sovereign uses violence, which is the state's exclusive privilege. In practice, we do not actually go this far, and as long as we do not, the Hobbesian solution is harder to justify. So although I am prepared, for now, to stick with the answers I have just offered, I must emphasize that I am a long way from being convinced that they are right, and, indeed, I think that if there is a flaw in the model that I am espousing, it comes precisely at this spot.

Disobedience and Violence (II)

Let me move for a moment from moral opposition to the murder of physicians at abortion clinics to moral opposition to the act of killing that a majority of American adults continue to insist is involved in abortion itself. Most Americans want abortion to be legal in most cases, but most Americans also think abortion is the killing of an entity that has a separate existence from the pregnant woman. Although there are certainly pro-life atheists (the journalist Nat Hentoff comes to mind), the leadership of the anti-abortion movement in America is principally motivated by an understanding of morality developed in religious communities. I mention this point because Christian theology carries a strong tradition of resistance to unjust laws. The church has long taught that unjust laws are not entitled to obedience—St. Augustine in particular refined this doctrine— but St. Thomas Aquinas went further, teaching that unjust laws are themselves acts of violence. Pope John Paul II, in his recent encyclical *The Gospel of Life*, quotes extensively from Aquinas in his frank effort to justify disobedience to constituted authority in the cause of preventing the enforcement of laws allowing abortion or euthanasia.[22] (He also criticizes, but with less rhetorical force, laws permitting capital punishment.)

Aquinas's point provides a useful inversion that is related to our inconclusive argument about the relative justifications for violence. When Aquinas argues that unjust laws are themselves acts of violence, he is only observing what in our statism we tend to miss: when the secular sovereign goes to enforce its laws, it does so with guns drawn.[23] One reason to be skeptical of state power is precisely this sad fact. The state—the secular sovereign—owns the weapons, the police, and the armed forces, and all of that apparatus can and often will be brought to bear on those who deny its sovereignty. The claim of serving a different sovereign, a claim absolutely essential to the Christian vision of disobedience, is one over which the secular sovereign is ultimately willing to kill.

I do not deny, of course, that sometimes the secular sovereign is justified in killing to enforce its laws. But the (potential) willingness of the secular sovereign to be violent in rejecting *all* claims of separate sovereignty is worrisome—understandable, but still worrisome. (Lest one think that the secular sovereign is not always prepared to kill disobedients, consider for a moment why it is that the police who make arrests always wear guns.)

From this perspective, it suddenly becomes much easier to understand the rhetoric of the "gun lobby," which drives liberal intellectuals half mad with its wholly implausible and yet somehow seamless argument that the gun in the household is the ultimate security for individual liberty. That argument is aimed at fears not of the escaped convict climbing in the bedroom window in the middle of the night but of the tanks rolling through the streets of town. When sufficiently fed with hate, that fear can lead to the ultimate horror, as we witnessed in April of 1995, when a 4,800-pound car bomb destroyed the Federal

Building in Oklahoma City, killing nearly two hundred people, many of them children. The accused bombers, according to news reports, had vague connections with the seemingly numberless private paramilitary organizations that stockpile weapons against what they consider an illegitimate and oppressive government regime. (Some of the groups, following the lead of the shadowy and extremely dangerous Christian Identity movement, have come to refer to the constituted American government as ZOG, for "Zionist Occupation Government.")

No political theory, no political or personal grievance can justify such wanton slaughter. And yet the Oklahoma City bombers differed from the many other violent resistance movements in our nation's violent history not in their vision of the government as the enemy, but only in the sophistication of their weapons and the soullessness with which they practiced their wicked craft. Much of the political violence in the nation's history has been in causes that were deemed of enormous importance at the political moment but that seem, in somber retrospect, quite trivial. Thus, one could now look back and say that the aforementioned 1798 armed revolt against the federal property tax was in a trivial cause. At times, these violent movements have even acted in what I at least would consider a good cause, such as John Brown's aforementioned raid on Harper's Ferry in a fruitless effort to spark an uprising among slaves. On some I am ambivalent. I have in mind, for example, the Black Panthers, who, alongside their sterling work of feeding the hungry and empowering the despised, counseled African Americans in the ways of armed self-defense. And some movements deserve ready and unstinting condemnation, which is where one would place the Ku Klux Klan in its days of greatest power and the far too numerous white supremacist groups of our unhappy era.

Today's white supremacist groups are linked by a peculiar

narrative of justice—or rather, injustice—in which citizens must arm themselves to be adequately defended against a government that will use force of arms to deprive them of their constitutional rights. There is a tragic negative synergy here, once one realizes that the principal right they believe to be at risk is their right to bear arms, the right they believe they are forced to exercise to prevent its infringement. And because the government is presumptively the enemy, it becomes natural, even rational, to shoot at and perhaps to kill law enforcement personnel who try to arrest the members of the community for violating the very laws that they have formed in order to protest.

One must not make the mistake of assuming that the violence and perhaps paranoia of these groups is an argument against the ideal of self-constituted communities; it is simply evidence, were any needed, that there is wickedness everywhere. And it should not be taken to bolster the terrifying yet specious arguments of the supremacists if one adds, as one is constrained by candor to do, that the underlying fears of the secular sovereign's potential for violence against disobedients are all too often borne out by events. Consider, for example, the use of real bullets to disperse anti-war protesters in the early 1970s, the use of police dogs to attack peaceful civil rights protesters a decade earlier, and, at the national level, the use of armed force to suppress the early trade union movement, most notably Grover Cleveland's sending soldiers for a military assault on the Pullman strikers in 1894—an episode, ironically, cited as precedent by the Eisenhower Administration in 1958, as it searched desperately for a legal rationale for sending troops to Little Rock to enforce a court order requiring desegregation. (In fact, it was the *only* precedent that a representative of the Justice Department, grilled by furious segregationist senators, was able to cite.)

And to the risk of murder at the hands of state functionaries one must add the traditional risk that the disobedient will face the lynch mob, for even when the secular sovereign ends up not killing those who claim to serve a different sovereign, an aroused local citizenry sometimes will do the job instead. This is quite famously true in the murders of scores of black Americans by mob violence between the end of the First Reconstruction in the 1870s and the successful conclusion of the legal structure of the Second in the 1960s. But those lynchings do not quite make the point, because they were killed precisely for insisting on their right of equal allegiance to the secular sovereign, not for the claim to serve another. Those who claimed to serve another sovereign were sometimes treated differently, as evidenced by the Ku Klux Klan's willingness to make at least a bit of common cause with Marcus Garvey's Universal Negro Improvement Association, which aimed in large measure at a "return" to Africa of American citizens whose skin happened to be black.

A better example of killing for the insistence on membership in a distinct community was the experience of Mormons and Roman Catholics, many of whom were murdered for their differences in the streets of American cities during the nineteenth century, including more than one riot sparked by a battle over the proper content of a prayer. Indeed, America's historical anti-Catholicism also served as justification for official violence by the secular sovereign, the national government—the violence, incredibly, of war. As the historian Paul Johnson writes: "In the McKinley-Roosevelt era, the Protestant churches were vociferous supporters of American expansion, especially at the expense of Spain, since they saw it as a God-determined process by which 'Romish superstition' was being replaced by 'Christian civilization.'"[24]

I count myself as one who believes that some of our potential for intolerance, along with the violence that it breeds, can be mediated by education. On this point John Dewey (whom, in the first lecture, I might have seemed to malign) was surely right. So was Horace Mann: if you want to build a good republic, you must first build good republicans. And you have to start early. Recently, a news magazine carried a heartbreaking photograph of a small boy—he was white—holding an automatic weapon and standing in front of the Confederate battle flag. Somebody certainly started early with him.

Of course, if we are to preach more tolerance, it is not sufficient to preach it to intolerant, divisive religionists, of which there are many; we must preach it as well to intolerant, divisive secular liberals, many of whom seem to value diversity across every spectrum except the religious. (Born-again Christians are woefully underrepresented at the nation's elite campuses, but when was the last time students or faculty organized to demand that more be hired?) Tolerance is not simply a willingness to listen to what others have to say. It is also a resistance to the quick use of state power—the exclusive prerogative of violent force, remember—to force dissenters and the different to conform. I do not think that Hannah Arendt was right in arguing that violence and power are opposites. I think my late Yale colleague Robert Cover had it right: power, by whatever name, *is* violence, violence implied if not violence committed.

That is why people with power have a moral obligation to be cautious rather than reckless in its exercise. In the first lecture, as we struggled to reinterpret the Declaration of Independence, I argued that the ultimate test of our democratic pretensions is the way we treat those whose dissent, whose acts of resistance to the sovereign's will, challenge our most cherished assumptions. I do not mean the violent, for the reasons I have been elucidating—I mean those who, as Dr. King used to say, are determined to make business as usual impossible. This is a greater problem for liberalism in the 1990s than it was in the 1960s because liberalism has won so many political battles in the intervening decades that it has developed a troubling moral complacency, particularly with respect to the tough questioning of authority that was once its glory. Demonstrations *against* liberal positions? Sit-ins? Non-violent resistance? Un-American! Get some new laws! RICO 'em! It is indeed a bit embarrassing, given the 1960s, but when today's political liberals talk about, say, protests at abortion clinics, one can hear, echoing down time's corridors, the terrifying logic of the silencing slogan of the silent majority days: "America—Love it or Leave It!" Which means, of course, "*Our* America—do it our way or go to jail!"

Disobedience and Definition

Having gone a good way down this somewhat anti-legal path, let us now retrace a bit of ground, taking a different turning to obtain a different view. After all, the decision on how to treat disobedience is also a part of the community's act of definition. In particular, the criminalizing of disobedience, quite apart from any question of deterrence, or even of signaling disapproval, may provide the community with crucial definitional moments. It is here that today's debates over whether to release from prison those whose offenses are non-violent overlook a key question—or perhaps presuppose its answer. What reason is there that the community's most intense definitional acts must draw their circles only around non-violence, screening only violence out? Might there not be other forms of definition, other screens that are, for particular communities, every bit as important, every bit as intense?

Consider, by way of example, the many colleges and universities that, during the 1980s, adopted regulatory codes governing what is sometimes called "hate speech." Critics of these rules, myself among them, questioned both their necessity and their wisdom, and many of the codes have since been challenged in court and struck down as unconstitutional or, in certain cases, as violations of state law.[25] And yet campus rules against hate speech, just like the seditious libel laws of the early Republic,[26] just like Lincoln's closing of newspapers that in his judgment impeded the war effort, just like the frequent legislative bans on a set of acts referred to loosely as vices, are all constitutive of a community. What act of self-definition could be stronger than the declaration that *People who say X are no part of us*? Surely Pope John Paul II does nothing different when he declares, in his recent encyclical on *The Gospel of Life*, addressed to "all the members of the Church," as follows: "In the case of an intrinsically unjust law, such as a law permitting abortion or euthanasia, it is . . . never licit to obey it, or to 'take part in a propaganda campaign in favour of such a law, or vote for it.'"[27] This, says the Pope, is what Roman Catholics must believe, and how they must act. He is attempting an act of definition, which every community has a right to do, and which, under the canons of the Catholic Church, the Pope unquestionably is called to do.

Remember the point we have already reviewed: self-constituted communities of meaning, unlike the Constitution-bound political sovereigns, may censor both the words and acts of their members. Members who do not like it, as we are reminded by Albert O. Hirschman in his well-known monograph *Exit, Voice, and Loyalty*, may protest or leave.[28] (The difficulty of leaving, and often of protesting, in political communities is an eminently sensible reason for placing constitutional limits on their ability to create conditions that make people want to.)

According to Hirschman, the dissatisfied are more likely to choose voice—his word for protest—if they believe that their complaints will make a difference in the behavior of the entity in question at relatively low cost to themselves. And the political sovereign must certainly take steps to assure that the many self-constituted communities in its midst do not use violence or other forms of coercion to bar exit, because that option must always be available if the communities are to be left alone. Some will choose to leave. But to stay in the face of one's own deeply felt objections—to stay after protest is rejected—is the ultimate act of loyalty, of willed and real allegiance to the community, for the self is then voluntarily submerged to the community's will—or, more properly, to the community's will as expressive of the meaning assigned by whatever source of authority the community respects.

So—to return to the principal example—I do not believe that the adoption of hate-speech regulations should be viewed principally as a constitutional question, for much the same reason that I think the Supreme Court did a great service to the ideal of community self-definition when it ruled that obscenity could be ascertained according to the standards of local communities (even though the communities it had in mind were of the arbitrary geographic variety that I have criticized). Although I happen to believe that hate-speech rules send a variety of troubling messages, I am reluctant to argue against the authority of a self-constituted campus community to impose them.

An additional word should be said about obscenity, which is often characterized as a "victimless crime." Quite apart from the feminist argument that we should think of pornography rather than obscenity as the relevant category and that pornography has its victims, both in its production and in its use, one must point out that it follows from the nature of community self-definition that the category of "victimless" crime cannot sensibly be said to exist; were there no victims, there would be no crime. The act of criminalization is itself a self-definitional act, and although it is often done in the name of the victims, it might more accurately be said to be done *by* the victims—for the community's lawgivers are a part of the community, and their judgments on what to forbid are ideally based on the prevention of harm to the whole but are at least based on the prevention of harm to themselves, even if the harm to themselves is a harm to their sensibilities.[29] Thus the labeling of a crime as victimless is actually an argument about epistemology: it is a claim that what the community defines as a harm is not properly classed as such. And in the epistemological system of the critic, this is no doubt true. But the critic's conclusion is only one side of the argument. A community that is unable to adopt and enforce its own vision of harm, based on its own epistemology, quickly ceases to be a community that can engage effectively in acts of self-definition.

I am not insisting that the ability of a community to define itself must be without limits. But in a society founded on a Declaration of Independence that warns against the rejection of the repeated petitions of the citizenry, those limits should be few, and we must avoid the totalizing tendency to treat all of our deeply held values as principles by which not only the national sovereign but every community, no matter how constituted, must be bound.

Dissent and Dialogue

More troubling theoretical and practical questions arise when the self-constituted community asks for more than the ability to set its own rules and determine, within broad limits, the fate of its own members. Sometimes, the community seeks instead to persuade the political sovereign to make rules to govern the conduct of individuals who are subject to the sovereign's will but not to the will of the self-constituted community. This occurs, for example, when religious activists seek to ban abortion. Efforts of this kind should be subject to the usual rules of democratic politics. When the efforts are pressed in morally wicked causes, they should be resisted; when they are pressed in morally worthy causes, they should be supported; but in neither case should it matter a jot whether the self-constituted communities pressing the secular sovereign to change happen to be religious in nature.

The reasons for this conclusion, which runs against the grain of much contemporary liberal political rhetoric, I and others have presented elsewhere.[30] (I also mentioned it in the first lecture.) I will not labor the point here, except to say that efforts to craft a public square from which religious conversation is absent, no matter how thoughtfully worked out, will always in the end say to the religionists that they alone, unlike everybody else, must enter public dialogue only after leaving behind that part of themselves that they may consider most vital. In the world of practical politics, where most Americans insist that their religious convictions are crucial to reaching moral and political decisions, dialogic rules that religious people experience as freezing them out will also continue the growing alienation from mainstream politics that I discussed in the first lecture, with no visible gain in return.

Very well, the religionists will be in the public square. What will ensue? Nowadays, many of our disputes over the effort of religious communities to influence the course of public discussion or public law involve the category of activities that liberal discourse lumps together, with no small degree of imprecision, as private. This is particularly true of our continuing battle over abortion and the more recent battle over the legal status of homosexual conduct.

Sexuality in its pure sense—whom one chooses to love and how one chooses to do it*—seems self-evidently private, both

---

*Nothing in this argument turns on whether one considers sexual orientation a matter of nature, nurture, choice, or some combination thereof.

in the traditional constitutional sense (the right to privacy as extending to activities the state cannot regulate except by vigorously intrusive means) and in our more difficult political-theoretical sense (the right to privacy as extending to a set of activities that, by their nature, individuals must be free to choose for themselves). So even though, for reasons I have already noted, it is foolish and historically naive to meet religious objections to homosexuality by asserting that religionists cannot impose their moral judgments on anybody else, it strikes me as fairly easy to meet the objections on the merits, that is, to defend the privacy right that covers sexual conduct. One triumphs, in other words, by doing that which I have stressed elsewhere is the only democratic way to meet religious claims of morality in the public square: to argue against them on the merits, by presenting the case for defeating them in terms independent of the religious source of the values in question.

As a scholar and citizen who is a Christian, I worry about the obsession of some members of my faith with rules to govern sexuality. This is true not only in the public debate that the liberal tradition believes to matter most but also in the very act of self-definition. For example (as I noted in the first lecture), the Southern Baptist Convention will withdraw fellowship from congregations that "affirm" homosexuality even though the SBC literally has listed *no* other moral or theological transgressions which will meet with the same sanction. My concern is that in both public debate and self-definition, the Christian tradition's strict rules on sexual conduct (which are today the subject of so much political controversy) may be overemphasized—not because sexuality does not need rules (it does), not because God doesn't care (God surely does), and not because popular mores have changed (that is the moment for the church to hold steadfast rather than shredding its traditions to please the crowd). The reason, rather, is that too often, in history and today, many churches have behaved as though the sexual appetite is the *only* appetite that might get out of control in the absence of hard-and-fast rules. There is not one deadly sin, there are seven, and contemporary Western society manages depressingly often to exemplify most of them.

Abortion, however, is quite a different matter, not least because the constitutional decisions of the Supreme Court in this area are so long on assertion and short on analysis. Consider just the most basic question in the abortion debate—whether the fetus is human—a question that drives true believers on both sides into something of a frenzy. In *Roe v. Wade*,[31] the Supreme Court ruled, for reasons it left largely unexplained, that the secular sovereign has no authority to enact legislation based on a particular answer to that question. The legal scholar Ronald Dworkin has lately defended that line of reasoning as celebrating the primacy of individual conscience, including the religious conscience, contending that the question of when life begins is irreducibly religious, and that therefore every pregnant woman, in the exercise of her own religious freedom, must be allowed to make the decision for herself.[32] Justice John Paul Stevens has accepted the reasoning of a number of legal scholars that it would violate the separation of church and state for the secular sovereign to enact an answer to this (again) irreducibly religious question.

But this clearly cannot be correct. If the state were not permitted to define the beginning of life, an individual whose children were already born could decide that they were not yet human beings and thus slay them—a point made by the philosopher Michael Tooley shortly after *Roe* was decided.[33] And even if the decision on when life begins *is* irreducibly religious, that hardly disables the state from acting. The state decides on when life begins for purposes ranging from income tax exemptions (surely the moment of birth is arbitrary for these purposes) to deciding whether one who kills a pregnant woman can be prosecuted for two murders or one. Indeed, the Court's own decision to allow the states to forbid abortion in the third trimester would seem to run against its own rule, once one recalls that the courts are an arm of the sovereign.

This leads to the second reason that abortion is different: in every significant philosophical system, and certainly in Christian theology, there is a vast distinction between allowing others to break a moral rule regarding personal sexuality and allowing others to break a moral rule protecting human life, which explains why *Evangelium Vitae* is a more compelling moral document than *Humanae Vitae*. Naturally, one may always answer the pro-life activist with the argument that the fetus is not a human being so the moral rule against taking innocent life therefore does not apply. But the argument is just that—an argument—and (even if one happens to agree with it) it is quite a bizarre one to elevate, as the Supreme Court has done, to a fundamental principle of constitutional law.

This does not mean that *Roe v. Wade* is wrong (although one would need a fresh justification to save it) or that the religious activists who seek to overturn it are right. It does mean that there is nothing about the *religious* source of their convictions that should bar them from public dialogue—a terrible rule, and one which, as I have mentioned, would have destroyed or severely disabled the moral arguments of both the Abolitionist movement and the civil rights movement. So the continuing battle for abortion rights should be fought on the merits of the rights in question, not on the ground that those who are against it have made up their minds according to a forbidden epistemology.

Again, Dissent and Witness

Even those who believe in the importance of abortion rights should see the usefulness to all of us of a continuing witness, even at the site of abortion clinics, to the possibility of fetal humanity—for that witness is itself a part of our public moral conversation. Let me here return for a moment to Pope John Paul II's encyclical *The Gospel of Life*. It clearly is not intended, and cannot fairly be read, as a justification for violence in the service of the Roman Catholic vision of life. But in its condemnation of the secular "culture of death," the encyclical clearly is intended, and must be read, as a justification for activism in the cause of life.

The encyclical is quite explicit: "Abortion and euthanasia are thus crimes which no human law can claim to legitimize. There is no obligation in conscience to obey such laws; instead there is a *grave and clear obligation to oppose them by conscientious objection*." The same is true even when one is simply asked to cooperate in the exercise of the abortion right by others: "To refuse to take part in committing an injustice is not only a moral duty; it is also a basic human right."[34]

If one is persuaded by John Paul II's argument, what form should the activism take? Putting violence to one side as, in my judgment, not morally supportable, the activism falls into two categories: *witness*, which can be as inoffensive as a prayer vigil or as intrusive as blocking the entrances of clinics; and *electoral politics*, by which I mean actually trying to gain control of the levers of secular power. Although a community may obviously do as it likes, I believe that in the special case of the religious community, a continuing moral witness is always superior to entrance into electoral politics.

Witness displays the religions at their best, as public moral critics, inspiring others by the power of rhetoric and example. It also allows the religions to remain pure in a particular sense: if uncorrupted by the trappings of secular authority, they will be better able to turn their critical moral attention to whatever ephemeral forces may be in charge. They will, moreover, be free of the political pressure to compromise that in the end reaches every political leader who declares himself or herself a person of true principle. And by remaining, at heart and in practice, as separate dissenting communities of meaning, the religions will be able to do what they must to continue: to meditate on and discuss the basic narrative traditions that provide their meanings, and to do it away from the temptations and incentives of the secular sovereign.

Electoral politics displays religions at their worst. One reason is that the very rhetoric of the divine that fires the religious commitment sounds arrogant and even hateful in the mouth of one who is driving for secular power. More important, religions that drive for secular power lose their best selves, for once one is able to tell others what to do, the incentive for inspiration disappears, replaced with the incentive for violence that is a characteristic of the secular sovereign, and so the religions begin the process of losing their souls. Let me here repeat what has often been said about the ultimate danger of the religious drive for political power, a danger not to politics but to the nature of religion itself: the inquisition became possible when the church gave up the power to die for its beliefs in exchange for the power to kill for its beliefs.

Again, Disobedience and the Courts

There remains the question of how the courts should treat those who are disobedient because of the commands of a separate sovereign, although the question need not long detain us now, as I will discuss it in the third and final lecture. For now, suffice it to say that we know that the courts are unsympathetic to civil disobedients in general, and the addition of a religious argument often makes matters worse rather than better. Not only do contemporary religious freedom plaintiffs fare badly; religionists who, in their disobedience, are seeking to change the existing laws of the secular sovereign often fare worse. One need not consider what I have already said about arrested members of Operation Rescue being forbidden to argue justice to the jury; just consider the Supreme Court's decision in *Walker v. City of Birmingham*,[35] sustaining the contempt citations issued against Martin Luther King and the other leaders of the Southern Christian Leadership Conference for parading in Birmingham on Good Friday and Easter Sunday without a permit and in defiance of a court order. Put aside the general question, of which I will say more in the third lecture, of whether the Court was correct to rule as it did, that a citizen generally may not raise constitutional arguments to explain the defiance of a court order. Just recognize that King and his fellow religionists had obvious religious reasons for wanting to march on Easter as against some other day—reasons the Justices treated as unimportant.

In this the Supreme Court was not at all aberrational. Our nation's refusal to acknowledge the category of political crime renders it difficult for the disobedient to explain to a court *why* the reasons are so important—unless the reasons sound in a familiar secular category, like running a red light to get to the hospital to perform a heart transplant. We have in American law and rhetoric only two categories of disobedients: those who are able to come up with a secular excuse for their lawbreaking and can therefore escape punishment, and those who are not and therefore cannot.

Still, it is unlikely that a lack of judicial sympathy will drive dissenting religious witness entirely underground. On the contrary, only rarely will religious beliefs held with such fervor remain secret. Instead, the courts will often make their decisions in the full knowledge that some, perhaps many, of those who are subject to them will be members of self-constituted communities of meaning and will, because they serve multiple sovereigns, feel constrained to disobey. One question we rarely pause to consider, but should probably think about more often, is whether it is ever appropriate for a judge called upon to decide a question of law to take into account this possibility—no, this likelihood—of disobedience. I ask only that you restrain your immediate answer of "Certainly not!" until the conclusion of the third and final lecture, in which I will spend time on the question.

The Dissent of the Governed

The principal point is that the way we conceive of dissent makes a difference in our rhetoric, our law, and our ability to create conditions in which communities of alternative meaning are able to flourish. That is why we must try to do the Declaration of Independence one better. Perhaps governments—good and fair ones, anyway—do not after all derive their powers from the *consent* of the governed. Perhaps they derive their powers instead from the *dissent* of the governed. For the fairness and democracy of any state should be assessed not alone through a study of whether its majorities examine it and find it good, but through a study of whether its minorities examine it and find it good. Another way to look at the matter is this: the justice of a state is not measured merely by its authority's tolerance for dissent, but also by its dissenters' tolerance for authority.

And if we believe, as I think we should, that more dissent is better than less, then we must find ways to clasp our many unruly yet non-violent disobedients to our hearts, even as we disagree, sometimes vehemently, with the causes they espouse. How, after all, can one have true allegiance to a secular state so totalizing that it is unable to tolerate action—not just belief, but action—that flows from the rich diversity of meanings that are developed in a flourishing culture of self-constituted communities? And if many, maybe most, of those communities are religious, and many of those religious communities challenge moral propositions to which we hold fast with great affection, surely we should view the process as a spur for important public moral dialogue rather than as a threat to our fundamental liberties.

Still, our own rhetoric confounds us. We are accustomed to describing these religious disobedients, with their irksome refusal to surrender their own vision of God's will for a secular vision of the will of man, as fanatics, fundamentalists, somehow directed by forces not amenable to reason. But this is simply a picture of the human condition, and it applies as easily, and as accurately, and with all the same strengths and weaknesses, to the political and legal systems within which the religious or non-religious disobedient struggles. One sees, on the part of the religious disobedients and the system that would crush them alike, a striving, a yearning, almost a desperation for the divine, seeking a vision not only of inerrancy, but of immutability: the rule is thus and cannot be other than thus and has never been other than thus. "The fool has said in his heart there is no God," wrote Aquinas, borrowing from scripture, and many philosophers have pilloried him for it. But sometimes we feel the same way about our religious disobedients: "The fool has said in his heart there is no law."

Of course, there is law—but our struggles over its meaning are often as baffling to the many self-constituted dissenting communities in our midst as their arcana of theology and morality are to the rest of us. Translation is not, thank God, impossible; but we often act as though it is undesirable. In the modern world of secular politics, enforcement is preferable to persuasion; for all the fine talk in our political philosophy about the virtues of conversation, nobody seems to have the time or the inclination to engage in any—not, at least, across the seemingly infinite and often trackless gulfs that divide our communities one from another. Far better to be able to say, simply, Do this—and have it done, like the servants of the centurion in the Gospel parable. That is the sense in which power tends to corrupt, even in a democracy: when one possesses power for too long, law becomes less the glue that knits us together than the name that we give to conclusions for which we would rather not offer arguments. The law need not be explained as long as it is spelled out (inerrantly) and obeyed (unquestioningly), for we *know* it to be right. That, of course, is the essence of what we have come to call fundamentalism, which is why fundamentalism may be simply another name for law.

3

Interpretation

IN THE FIRST two lectures, I have discussed the ways that our notions of allegiance and dissent may interfere with the ability of communities of meaning—particularly religious communities—to thrive or even to survive, especially if those communities share visions of reality that are at sharp variance with the vision of the dominant political community. At the same time, in styling these lectures a "meditation," I have disclaimed, in large measure, any law reform ambitions. But I am, of course, a law professor, and so the disclaimer eventually must collapse, and I suppose today is the day. Because in this third lecture, I will address with some precision what I have only hinted at over the past two afternoons: the role of the courts in establishing the way that we as a society confront the dissent of the governed. And when one discusses the role of the courts, one inevitably shades into suggesting what judges *should* do. And so I shall.

Let me offer a bit of a roadmap, for we will be discussing what may seem three sharply different subjects, although I hope to be able, by the end, to tie them together.

First, we will consider the ways in which judges are uneasy about the fact that they are a part of the sovereign, which results in an inability to deal effectively with the loving disobedience of (for example) a Martin Luther King, disobedience that falls well short of disallegiance to the nation. Like the rest of us, the courts prefer to pretend that they are a check on the state rather than a part of the state, but they are far more the second than the first. The best evidence of this is the way in which judges, as though worried that their orders might be defied, indulge in a rhetoric that sometimes makes it impossible for the reader to tell when they are talking about civil disobedients and when they are talking about traitors. The distinction seems to come especially hard when the disobedients in question are standing up to the judges because their religious consciences tell them that they must, which is one reason that judges should work hard, as I suggested in the second lecture, to find ways to accommodate the needs of religionists to be different.

This leads to a second problem: ever since the civil rights era, Americans have been taught that it is a deep and fundamental wrong to defy the courts, wronger somehow than breaking a law passed by the legislature. Unfortunately, this has led the courts to greater hubris rather than greater humility in interpreting the Constitution, as though the fact that disobedience is unlikely means that the judges are free to do whatever they wish. Missing in the current debate over constitutional method is the wisdom of the late Alexander Bickel, who warned back in the 1960s that judicial legitimacy is found in the link between how courts reach their decisions and why people obey them.

Third, we will examine, albeit briefly, the tantalizing possibility that courts should pay more attention than they do to popular dissatisfaction with their rulings, not merely because the judges are not the sole repositories of wisdom, but also because, as part of the sovereign, the judicial branch, too, must be responsive to the repeated petitions of an aroused citizenry. My examples, once more, will be drawn largely from the confrontations between law and religion, for these unruly religionists often refuse to accede to the decree of the secular sovereign, even when that sovereign speaks through the putatively neutral voice of its courts. Of course, any sensitivity to the concern of the disobedients must be balanced against the ordinary understanding of the judicial function. Although the balance is a difficult one to strike, and I have neither the space nor the wisdom to offer a full solution here, a judiciary that refuses even to try necessarily contributes to the growing popular image of a sovereign that is, quite literally, out of control.

In all of this, my principal goal is to reflect on the difficulty that judges have in accepting the religious world view as one that can possibly guide a just and sensible citizen, and the consequent judicial intolerance of the disobedience that religion sometimes makes necessary. I hope to continue to find echoes of our reconstruction of the Declaration of Independence during the first afternoon of these lectures. The courts, after all, are a part of the sovereign, and so when we contemplate the way in which the sovereign responds to the "repeated Petitions" of citizens who are profoundly unhappy, and the implications of that response for successful democracy, we can hardly leave out the judges.

Dr. King in the Sovereign's Courts

I would like to begin with an observation about the courts—an aspect of the courts that all of us know but that few of us, in our rhetoric, like to talk about. The observation is this: the courts are a part of the government. They are, in other words, not a *check on* the sovereign but a *part of* the sovereign, and this is true whether you imagine the American sovereignty to reside in the people, their representatives, or anyplace else. So all the fine talk about "judicial review" as a way to test the actions of a thing called "the government" or "the state" against another thing called "the Constitution" is often little more than that: fine talk. One does better to be more cautious, to view executive-judicial or legislative-judicial disputes as family arguments. Because, at the end of the day, the branches of government are stuck with one another in a particular sense: all three share an interest in the survival of constituted authority.

I begin with these observations for a reason. In the second lecture, I spoke about Martin Luther King's eloquent "Letter from Birmingham City Jail." It is, of course, a crucial document in American political history. Every educated American knows it, or should. But consider a single, simple question: What, precisely, was Dr. King *doing* in the Birmingham city jail? How did he get there—and how did the way he got there relate to the contents of the letter?

If you consult the popular histories (and many of the serious histories as well) you will quickly learn that Dr. King and other leaders of the 1963 march in Birmingham were jailed for parading without a permit. But this description is, at best, imprecise; to the serious student of law or history, it is woefully misleading. Dr. King and the others were in jail for contempt of court, the result of violating a *court order* commanding them not to march without a permit—a distinction that might appear historically trivial, but one that is, for our purposes, analytically crucial.

One must try to visualize the atmospherics of Birmingham in 1963, the defiant civil rights marchers against the determined segregationist city fathers. When official and unofficial forms of intimidation proved insufficient to deter the members of the Southern Christian Leadership Conference from marching in protest on Good Friday and Easter Sunday, the city rushed to a local judge and obtained a temporary restraining order (TRO) prohibiting the parade. The petition for the injunction hinted at mobs, lawlessness, and other threats to "the safety, peace and tranquility of the City." The judge issued the order *ex parte*— that is, without hearing argument from the other side.

Upon receiving notice of the TRO, King issued a statement that anticipated the argument he would later make in the more famous "Letter": "This is raw tyranny under the guise of maintaining law and order. We cannot in all good conscience obey such an injunction which is an unjust, undemocratic and unconstitutional misuse of the legal process." He went on to say of his group's planned defiance: "We do this not out of any disrespect for the law but out of the highest respect for *the* law. This is not an attempt to evade or defy the law or engage in chaotic anarchy. Just as in all good conscience we cannot obey unjust laws, neither can we respect the unjust use of courts. We believe in a system of law based on justice and morality."

King, then, refused to accept the fiction that the courts are not a part of the sovereign, or that their decrees should be judged by a different moral standard than the pronouncements of the executive or the legislature. Indeed, had he believed otherwise, his act of civil disobedience would have lost some of its moral force. After all, King was protesting the law requiring segregation, not the law forbidding parading without a permit—but it was the second (presumptively just) law that he broke. The moral connection is created by his insistence that the courts are bound by the same standards as any other part of the sovereign. Thus the court order forbidding the breaking of the ordinance was fairly subject to moral (that is, religious) criticism, whether or not the underlying law against parading was. The decision to march without a permit then becomes a protest, not against segregation as such, but *against the court order*. For the court order was the illegitimate instrument of the immoral system of segregation.

The rest of the story is instructive. After announcing his intention to defy the court order, King asked for volunteers to march and go to jail. Without a permit, and in defiance of the TRO, they marched on Good Friday. They were not arrested. They marched again on Easter Sunday. They were not arrested. On Monday morning, the marchers were hauled before the judge to face charges of criminal contempt—not for violating the statute, but for violating the court order. They were convicted and sentenced to five days in jail and a $50 fine apiece. They appealed, but the Alabama Supreme Court upheld the contempt citation.

When the case—now known as *Walker v. City of Birmingham*—at last reached the Supreme Court, the principal issue was whether, at the contempt hearing, the marchers should have had the opportunity to argue that the order was a violation of their First Amendment rights.[1] Ordinarily, when a defendant wants to challenge a law as unconstitutionally burdening his freedom of speech, he may first violate the law and then, when placed on trial, raise the constitutional argument as an affirmative defense. That is what the marchers tried to do here. But the judge who had issued the order refused to listen: the only question, he ruled, was whether or not his order had been violated. Because the marchers obviously could not deny the violation, they went to jail; which is how the "Letter" came to be written.

In historical context, the point is an important one. King's critics were not, as we tend to think today, attacking him simply for breaking the law. They were attacking him for violating a court order—which, elsewhere in the South, the litigation wing of the civil rights movement was arguing that everybody *must* obey, whether or not the order is popular.* This, indeed, was the point of *Cooper v. Aaron*,[2] the Supreme Court's decision in the Little Rock desegregation case, which I mentioned in the first lecture and about which I will shortly say an additional word. Across the country, the civil rights litigators were arguing that a respect for law and order required obedience to the courts—or, more properly, that disobeying the courts was the same as a lack of respect for law and order. Just a few years earlier, Thurgood Marshall, then head of the NAACP Legal Defense Fund, had warned that failure to heed the rulings of the Supreme Court would be the end of America.

So King, in his "Letter from Birmingham City Jail," was

---

*Today, conservative critics of the pro-life group Operation Rescue, whose members sometimes break the law by blockading the entrances to abortion clinics, also argue that disobedience is not an appropriate means of making a political point.

writing his way out of a paradox. That is why he takes pains in the letter to distinguish the loving disobedience that he preaches from the "white mothers . . . in New Orleans . . . screaming 'nigger, nigger, nigger'";[3] and that is why he is at equal pains to argue that a loving disobedience, along with a willingness to accept the penalty, demonstrates the highest respect for law. King, in short, was not writing an abstract discourse on civil disobedience; he was, as his "Letter" shows, quite conscious of the arguments over disobedience that were taking place around him.

The courts, too, were doubtless aware of what was going on around them, but they wrote as though only abstract principle was involved. This is how the Supreme Court described the principle on which the state court relied in holding the marchers in contempt: "The rule of law that Alabama followed in this case reflects a belief that in the fair administration of justice no man can be judge in his own case; however exalted his station, however righteous his motives, and irrespective of his race, color, politics, or religion." And the very last words of Justice Stewart's opinion for the majority are as tragic as they are telling: "One may sympathize with the petitioners' impatient commitment to their cause. But respect for judicial process is a small price to pay for the civilizing hand of law, which alone can give abiding meaning to constitutional freedom."[4] And what did the Justices mean by "respect for judicial process"? They meant that a court order, even a seemingly unconstitutional one, cannot be disobeyed—that the courts are simply not like other branches of government. If the order is unconstitutional, the person who is the subject of the order must obey it nevertheless, and challenge it later.

Yet the importance of the Court's opinion in *Walker* does not lie only in its refusal to allow the marchers to offer constitutional justifications for their disobedience. This, at least, could plausibly be defended as the teaching of the precedents. The more troubling problem is that by counseling the marchers to wait and challenge the order later, the Court gave no weight whatever to the religious narrative that led to the disobedience, even though the Justices would have had to be willfully blind to miss the significance of marching on Good Friday (sacrifice) and Easter Sunday (resurrection).[5] But the blindness may have been less because of the marchers' religiosity than because of the Court's determination to protect itself: had the disobedients' excuse been taken seriously, the entire project of liberal constitutionalism that I mentioned in the first lecture would have been at hazard. Why? Because that project rests on the foundational point that the courts are far wiser than anybody else (sovereign or citizen) and thus must be obeyed, always and everywhere and by everyone. Period.

Again, Disobedience

Let us go back a step. We saw in the first lecture that the justice of the sovereign may be judged in part on how it treats the repeated petitions of dissatisfied citizens. That was the point of our reinterpreted Declaration of Independence. In other contexts, the courts seem to understand this. Thus, the First Amendment has been crafted into a powerful tool for the protection of citizens seeking to disobey the unconstitutional edicts of every other agency of government. When an unconstitutional statute is violated, for example, the courts refuse to allow any punishment. If the rights the statute infringes are free speech rights, the courts warn of the "chilling effect" of such laws. But if those same free speech rights are infringed instead by court order, the failure to punish disobedience is suddenly a fundamental threat to the rule of law—and thus to the sovereign itself.

The courts are sometimes almost strident on the point. We

have already reviewed Justice Stewart's closing words for the Supreme Court in *Walker v. City of Birmingham*. When you have the time, go back and read the Court's opinions in *Cooper v. Aaron* and *United States v. Nixon*,[6] both of which were produced by jurists keenly aware of the possibility of official disobedience. *Cooper*, which produced the unprecedented vision of an opinion signed by all nine Justices, commanded immediate integration of Little Rock High School, and was written in direct response to the defiant words of segregationist Governor Orval Faubus of Arkansas, who had suggested that his own interpretation of the Constitution was entitled to as much weight as the Court's. *United States v. Nixon*, a unanimous opinion written by Chief Justice Warren Burger, required President Nixon to surrender to the special prosecutor recordings of conversations relating to the Watergate cover-up, and was drafted in the face of the Court's certain knowledge of two points: first, that the President had hinted quite publicly that he might defy anything other than a "definitive" opinion; and, second, that the Watergate grand jury had secretly named the President as an unindicted co-conspirator.

The *Nixon* opinion, although conceding the importance of the President's claim that the recordings were protected by executive privilege, warned that "this presumptive privilege must be considered in light of our historic commitment to the rule of law," and added that the precedent of the *Burr* case[7]—in which Chief Justice John Marshall implied that a subpoena directed to the President might not be enforceable—"cannot be read to mean in any sense that a President is above the law." In other words, if President Nixon dared defy the Court, he would be placing himself beyond the rule of law—that is, the law as spoken by the judges.

This resistance to the idea of disobedience, although perfectly understandable as a matter of political science, places the courts in the awkward position of being among the rejecters of the "repeated Petitions" of which the Declaration speaks. Naturally, no more than (exactly) half of litigants can actually win, and many of the losers must be among those who are challenging the sovereign. (Even excluding criminal cases, governments win far more lawsuits than they lose.) Yet popular rhetoric about the courts suggests that they are places to which citizens can repair for redress when the "government"—again, somehow defined as excluding judges—has denied them their rights.

Nevertheless, it should be plain that courts cannot really play this role. Remember what I pointed out earlier, and what Dr. King never forgot—that the courts are simply an arm of the state. But they are not like the other arms, and the judges know it. And the ways in which they are different help explain why, in cases of genuine dissensus, the judiciary cannot operate as a significant check on the other branches.

How is being a judge different? But for our post-civil-rights love affair with judicial power, the answer would be obvious. A judge can tell people what to do, but the people might not do what they are told. And if the people refuse to do what they are told, there is little that the judge can do about it—not, at least, without the aid of another, more powerful branch of government. The legal scholar Arthur Leff once wrote that behind every judicial decision stands the massed might of the 82nd Airborne.[8] But Leff was writing tongue-in-cheek, for he plainly recognized that the claim is not quite true. The 82nd Airborne stands behind the judicial opinion only if the troops are ordered to go—and a judge cannot give that order.

The simple truth is that judges have few weapons other than their own prestige with which to force compliance with their edicts. Alexander Bickel pressed this point quite eloquently a generation ago, but today's constitutional theorists seem to find it a little bit embarrassing.[9] Nowadays, legal scholars rarely try to link theories of adjudication to theories of political obligation. The shelves of the nation's law libraries are lined with sophisticated arguments on why judges should adopt one interpretive approach or another when confronting constitutional questions, but very few of the authors bother to explain why, if the judge follows the method advocated, anybody should pay attention. Smart scholars have argued for constitutional rights to everything from health care to drug use to nonpayment of taxes, and some of the arguments are quite engaging; but constitutional theory, as a body, gives inadequate attention to what it is that turns a judicial "opinion," as a court's written product is so honestly called, into a lawgiving event.

Not only is constitutional theory embarrassed by this omission—so are the judges themselves. True, judicial opinions almost never make explicit reference to the possibility of disobedience; and, when they do, it is almost always in condemnation, as one would expect. The thundering anathema at the very idea of defiance has worked its way into our political language, I suspect, largely because of its relentless repetition by the courts which, during the civil rights era, millions of Americans sensibly came to love. But the fact that judges express no doubts that their decisions (that is, opinions) will be obeyed should not be taken to mean that they harbor none. And there are, from time to time, moments of quite astonishing judicial honesty. One is the Supreme Court's 1867 decision in *Mississippi v. Johnson*,[10] in which the Justices declined to issue an order prohibiting President Andrew Johnson from enforcing the Reconstruction Acts. The stated ground was enchantingly straightforward: "If the President refuse obedience, it is needless to observe that the court is without power to enforce its process."

But such frank discussions of judicial weakness are rare events, even though we have known, at least since the pioneering work of Bickel in the sixties, of the many indirect ways in which judges incorporate into their opinions their self-knowledge of weakness. Bickel pointed out that the courts often use such amorphous doctrines as standing, justiciability, mootness, and ripeness to avoid deciding those things they would rather not decide—and that the prudence of deciding not to decide is often a matter of preserving scarce judicial capital for the next (perhaps more important) battle.

Contemporary scholars look askance at Bickel, who is seen as misunderstanding the judicial responsibility to decide questions properly put. To the bloodless technocrat, this may seem to be precisely right. To the ruthless promoter of causes, Bickel may even seem a bit reactionary, not to say cowardly. But today's theorists often forget that Bickel pointed to the inherent weakness of the judiciary in order to *defend* the courts against mainstream critics who considered the desegregation decision an illegitimate power-grab: the courts, he meant his readers to understand, were not "dangerous." Bickel's genius came in his recognizing what modern theory would rather ignore: it is not obvious that people will obey judicial opinions that are wrongheaded, and even less obvious that they should. The "passive virtues," as Bickel called them, enable the courts to avoid squandering their legitimacy by seeming to find constitutional rights everywhere. Or they did perform that function, in the days when judicial hubris was less than it is now.

Disobedience Redux

Of course, the judicial concern for disobedience is not a concern only about the edicts of the courts. Judges, as part of the sovereign, view with displeasure any efforts to thwart the sovereign's will, unless the defendants are able to convince the judges that their efforts are in furtherance of a higher *constitutional* goal. Indeed, interesting cases involving organized defiance most frequently arise when the defendants offer a claim of constitutional right—and, when the claim is rejected, frequently spark near-hysterical judicial rhetoric on the virtues of obedience.

In cases involving religious disobedients, the pitch of judicial rhetoric is particularly fevered. For example, in *Reynolds v. United States*,[11] a unanimous Supreme Court made short work of the claim that the religious freedom of Mormons permitted them to engage in polygamous marriage in violation of an 1862 federal law that made plural marriage a felony—notwithstanding that the law was clearly directed against the Church of Latter-Day Saints as such. (The law also dissolved the church's charitable incorporation.) To allow the Mormons to do what their religion encouraged would be, said the Justices, "subversive of good order." So Mormons who followed church teaching in the matter of plural marriage were, in so many words, subversives.

In this connection, it is useful to compare the language chosen by Justice Stewart in the *Walker* case, which, you will recall, sustained the contempt citation of Martin Luther King Jr., with the language chosen a quarter-century later by Justice Antonin Scalia in *Employment Division v. Smith*,[12] which sustained the refusal of the state of Oregon to grant employment compensation to two Native Americans who were fired from their state job because they used peyote in a religious ceremony older than the anti-drug laws. Although the *Smith* case, unlike *Walker*, did not concern disobedience to a court order, the similarity between the two cases is greater than the difference, for in both cases it was the force of religious belief that moved the petitioning citizens to their disobedience—and following forceful religious conviction, as we saw in the second lecture, is often very much like serving a separate sovereign.

With this prospect the courts, so sensitive on the question of sovereignty, can hardly be happy. Remember the line from

Walker we heard earlier: "In the fair administration of justice no man can be judge in his own case, however exalted his station, however righteous his motives, and irrespective of his race, color, politics, or religion." Why? Because "respect for judicial process is a small price to pay for the civilizing hand of law, which alone can give abiding meaning to constitutional freedom."

Now consider the words of Justice Scalia a quarter-century later: "It may fairly be said that leaving accommodation to the political process will place at a relative disadvantage those religious practices that are not widely engaged in; but that unavoidable consequence of democratic government must be preferred to a system in which each conscience is a law unto itself."[13] Both opinions refer, with open dismay, to the prospect of allowing us (in context, the religiously disobedient us) to be laws unto ourselves. Not only is the language of the two opinions similar but the basic point is in both cases the same: the law is the law, and minorities that believe themselves mistreated have no privilege, in their impatience, to defy it. They may file and file their repeated petitions—but rebuffing those petitions is evidently an obligation of the judicial craft.

In short, citizens who cite religious grounds when they defy the democratically enacted laws that apply to everybody else are not simply lawbreakers, although they obviously are that too; they are, in some peculiar sense, placing their will in opposition to the General Will (as Rousseau called it) and are therefore actively working against the sovereign. And if all of this sounds like the language of treason, the reason is that the ways the courts talk about traitors and the ways the courts talk about disobedients are, unfortunately, quite similar.

Disobedience, Treason, and Capital Punishment

Treason, the only criminal offense defined in the Constitution, is a capital offense, which means that the state can kill for it.

And the constitutional definition of treason is, in the present context, quite fascinating: "Treason against the United States, shall consist only in levying War against them, or in adhering to their Enemies, giving them Aid and Comfort." What is serving a separate sovereign if not "adhering" to it? And, if that separate sovereign commands a set of meanings different from those imposed by the secular state, it is obviously an "enemy." Thus it should hardly be any surprise that the language courts and politicians use to discuss those accused of treason has historically been quite similar to the language they use to discuss those accused of adhering to their religious rather than secular sovereigns.

Consider where the law of treason comes from. In the Anglo-American tradition, its source is the first English criminal statute, which outlawed "compassing the death of the king"—that is, planning to kill him—because, as Professor George Fletcher points out, intending to kill the king "breaches the duty of fealty required under the feudal system"—that is, the trade of feudal loyalty for royal protection.[14] That bargain, of course, is at the heart of the Hobbesian contract that underlies our contemporary understanding of sovereignty: individuals gain security, but make themselves subject to the will of the sovereign. Thus, our contemporary vision of treason stresses not intention but action. The Constitution requires an "overt act" because some English authorities argued in perfect sincerity that disloyal *thoughts* were treasonous. (Of course, several of the rebellious colonies made it a crime to *express* support for George III.) The law of treason, in short, matches the speech/ action or belief/action distinctions that we examined in the second lecture, in discussing the case of the anarchist Benjamin Gitlow.

Gitlow was what was in those days called a subversive—like the Mormons who practiced plural marriage, he was a threat to good order, because he served a different sovereign. Still, one does not want to carry the analogy too far. Treason in its political sense is considered a far more serious offense than religiously motivated defiance of most laws, and the penalty is naturally different too. The Native Americans involved in the *Smith* case were simply refused unemployment compensation; Dr. King spent a few days in jail. Traitors face capital punishment. But although America has lynched Jews, Roman Catholics, and Mormons, it has never adopted a statute allowing their execution.

The American public, in its more sober moments, is sensitive to the risks of this willingness to kill for adherence to a separate sovereign. When the Jeffersonians impeached Justice Samuel Chase in 1805, and came very close to gaining enough Senate votes to remove him from office, one of the charges was that in the trial of John Fries, the decidedly uncivil disobedient who took up arms against the federal property tax, Chase had bent over backward to persuade the jury to convict the defendant of the charge of treason, which carried with it the possibility of execution.[15] And, in a remarkable and in some ways troubling display of compassion, the Union, after its victory in the Civil War, winded up staging only a tiny handful of treason trials. Even Jefferson Davis, the president of the Confederacy, escaped trial following his indictment for treason when, along with the rest of those who fought for the South, he was pardoned by President Andrew Johnson in 1868.

On the other hand, in the most famous treason case of this century, the public seemed to line up in favor of swift and certain punishment. I refer to the Rosenberg trial. Even today, one can provoke heated argument among American intellectuals of a certain generation by expressing a strong opinion on the guilt or innocence of Julius and Ethel Rosenberg, accused of stealing the secret of the hydrogen bomb for the Soviet Union. Although, as a formal matter, the Rosenbergs were charged with espionage (they turned out to be the last Americans ever executed for that offense), the tone of the trial, and of the commentary, sounded very much in treason.[16]

Ideally, when the secular sovereign decides to try a citizen on a charge that amounts to serving a separate sovereign, the jury should be pressed toward the sobriety of democratic respect rather than the intoxicating fury of the witch-hunt. For just this reason, it is absolutely vital to the project of community preservation that counsel for the accused be allowed to argue to the jury on the justice of the statute that the disobedient disobeyed. Once upon a time, for example in the John Peter Zenger case,[17] the importance of allowing such arguments was well understood in American practice. Nowadays, unfortunately, the trend is very much in the other direction. Judges routinely forbid it. For example, the members of the pro-life activist group Operation Rescue, when tried on criminal charges, routinely seek and are routinely refused permission to argue to the jury on their reasons for believing abortion unjust. Perhaps, were they allowed to make the argument, the jury would disagree; but to say that they should not be allowed to try is simply undemocratic. And here I mean undemocratic in the very specific sense that I mentioned in the first lecture: tending to presume the absolute justice of the will of the secular sovereign.

Of course, juries may go into the matter even in the absence of any argument from counsel. News accounts suggested that the jury that tried District of Columbia Mayor Marion Barry on drug charges discussed the propriety of the prosecution's conduct before convicting Barry of a lesser charge. And during the jury proceedings of the Chicago Seven Trial in 1970, jurors debated the constitutionality of the anti-rioting statute that formed the backbone of the government's case, even though counsel for the defense had requested and been refused permission to argue the point to the jurors.[18] But there is no reason to think that this ordinarily takes place.

Opponents of what has come to be called jury nullification like to cite the horrors of, for example, the trials of white supremacists in the South during the middle years of the twentieth century: no jury, it seemed, would convict whites for crimes against blacks. But, of course, this is no argument at all, for racist juries will release racist criminals whether argument about justice is allowed or not; we should be about as comfortable arguing against free speech on the ground that some free speakers are bigots. It is very much in the nature of the tools of democratic dissent that they may be used by the bad guys as well as the good guys. Nullification may be viewed as a response by one's fellow citizens to the dissenting petitions that, as we have seen, a true democracy must be willing to hear. Thus the tool of nullification is a necessary one, unless one presumes that a given state is more likely than a given jury to choose the correct moral answer.

Bear in mind (as I mentioned in the second lecture) that the big question in the philosophy of civil disobedience has always been whether the civil disobedient has an obligation to own up to what he is doing, to take a public stance and suffer the consequences. In other work, I have suggested an answer to this classic question, but my answer, I admit, has always struck me (and others) as something of a straddle. My answer in the past has been that the disobedient who accepts the basic justice of his society has a presumptive obligation to be open and public, whereas the disobedient who rejects the basic justice of his society has no such obligation.[19] I freely admit that I now find my earlier answer somewhat unsatisfying, because it is too categorical. Disobedience, surely, is a creative act, and the question of punishment deserves a creative answer.

But whatever may be the right solution to the puzzle of when civil disobedients are morally obligated to face punishment, the judicial refusal to allow disobedients to argue to the jury on the justice of the underlying cause is bound to create a disincentive for being open in disobedience. One common goal of the open disobedient is to turn the trial into a forum on his or her cause. If, in our turn to statism, we refuse to allow argument of this kind, there is much less point to the open and loving disobedience that so much of our moral philosophy once celebrated and that the public ministry of the Reverend Martin Luther King Jr. so powerfully epitomized, and there is more reason than ever for the disobedient to shirk both moral and legal responsibility.

At this point, I must once more repair to constitutionalism, for the temptation is surely to reply to my argument with the assertion that our system does not presume the absolute justice of the will of the sovereign. It is possible, after all, to appeal one's case to the constitutional courts. But the availability of judicial review creates only the illusion that the will of the secular sovereign is subject to challenge. Remember that the judges themselves, although they write as though it were not so, are functionaries of the secular sovereign. And when they cite the various clauses of the Constitution as justifications for their decisions, they are able to do so and be obeyed precisely because their claim is that they are enforcing the *true* will of the *higher* sovereign—the sovereign compact of We, the People, as represented in the Founding Document.[20] Indeed, the often oracular nature of the relationship of the Justices to the public probably reinforces, rather than ameliorating, the vision of a single and essentially omnipotent sovereign.

Moreover, as the late Robert Cover pointed out, judges are themselves creatures of violence, for lurking behind their decrees is violence both metaphorical and physical: metaphorical because judges are what Cover calls jurispathic, using law to destroy the narrative traditions that interfere with their visions of justice; and physical because the judges can order the arrest and imprisonment of those who disagree with their edicts.[21] In battles between the sovereign on one hand, and the individual or group on the other, this characteristic matters. The judges may command fewer forces of violence than other parts of the secular sovereign do, but they certainly command more than does the disobedient. And if judges happen to order executions, as they did in the Rosenberg case, the executive will usually, and with no visible reluctance, carry them out.

Please do not misunderstand my purpose. I am not defending traitors. I simply wish that our courts would recognize the crucial role of dissensus in our polity and thus, when facing incidents of disobedience that constitute less than treason, would avoid language suggesting that all disobedients are somehow compassing the death of the king.

Disobedience and Interpretation

I emphasized earlier that the courts are a branch of the sovereign, not a check on it, a point that Martin Luther King Jr. explicitly recognized in his Easter weekend disobedience. This means that when the courts act disdainfully toward disobedients, a part of the sovereign is rejecting the repeated petitions of the citizen. The most obvious reason is that the courts are not drawing people into dialogue, but are instead ordering them about—an aspect of judicial process that conservatives celebrated, for example, with the passage of the Taft-Hartley Act at the midpoint of the century, and which liberals, who want to stop anti-abortion protests, not labor strikes, celebrate today. Citizens who have been raised to think that they are self-governing can hardly be expected to enjoy the celebration.

In the particular situation of religious disobedients, courts that so readily reject the repeated petitions for redress may also be acting in defiance of the text and history of the Constitution.

Many scholars and some judges have argued that the Free Exercise Clause of the First Amendment often requires the sovereign to grant religious disobedients a special exemption from laws that apply to everybody else. The literature calls this an accommodation of religious belief.

The classic example of an accommodation claim—one, in fact, that the Supreme Court long ago upheld—involves a religious disobedient who is prosecuted for violating a local law against door-to-door solicitation. The disobedient responds that she is a Jehovah's Witness, and is required by the tenets of her religion to go from one house to the next to raise funds.[22] One vision of the separation of church and state would hold that it is unconstitutional to exempt religious groups from laws of general application. For no good reason, this vision is referred to as neutralist. (It isn't at all neutral: the disobedient loses the case by definition.) The accommodationist vision, by contrast, holds that there are times when religious freedom is impossible unless an exemption is granted.

Accommodationists, in fact, frequently argue that the text and history of the Constitution itself mandate special exemptions. This is not the place to get into that debate (I have gotten into it elsewhere),[23] except to note that the heart of the historical case is the proposition that religious freedom at the time of the founding simply meant being left alone to profess and practice one's faith, but that we nowadays live in a society that leaves almost no aspect of life alone. The United States is a regulated society, and our national instinct is to resolve whatever crises arise by enacting more laws. There is little if any truly unregulated space, which means that government treads constantly on religious exercise. Consequently—so the argument runs—in order to translate the Framers' vision of religious freedom into one that works in the regulated world, we must create spheres in which religions will not be regulated even though other things are. In this way, we create functional equivalents of the freedom to be left alone to profess and practice the faith.[24]

Of course, this argument will have appeal only to an interpreter who believes that text and history matter; and to argue for accommodations on grounds of text and history is to take a position in the age-old struggle over how to determine what the Constitution "means." To politicians, and to many citizens, what the Constitution means is whatever a particular political movement needs it to mean: to oversimplify a bit, liberals know that the document protects the right to an abortion (goodness knows where) and conservatives know that it outlaws affirmative action (goodness knows how). Constitutional theorists make their livings by insisting that matters are a bit more complicated. The debate is a large and important one; for present purposes, I will mention only one small corner, a corner that is closely related to our larger subject of the dissent of the governed. To explain why, I will need to digress in ways that some might find didactic, but which, I assure you, are necessary.

Consider: One might argue that the history of the First Amendment does not really matter—or that the text does not really matter—or that the project that the Framers thought they were engaged in does not really matter. One might argue that all that really matters is finding the right principle and then fitting it into whatever constitutional clause most plausibly makes it work. Where that "right principle" comes from—well, that has always been the puzzle of modern constitutional law. If the relevant principle is the view of the majority (what "we" think, as the courts like to say, with no apparent sense of irony), then constitutional courts are scarcely needed, and certainly will be unable to do the work of protecting the minority. But if the principle is simply chosen from a particular system of moral philosophy that the judge happens to favor, then the judge's theory of adjudication does not pass even the first test that I mentioned: there is no obvious reason that anybody ought to obey.

Most theorists who bother to express an opinion tell us that the people should obey for Lockean reasons: having accepted the benefits of citizenship, they can hardly dismiss the burdens. But this is only part of an answer. What makes obedience to a particular court decision a burden of citizenship? Well, we should know that: the Constitution does. That is, the Constitution both establishes the institution of judicial review (the old saw that the Framers never anticipated it was long ago discredited) and sets forth the rules that the judiciary may use to bind the other branches. As the historian Michael Kammen reminds us in his wonderful book *A Machine That Would Go of Itself*,[25] Americans have always revered the Constitution, in large part because of a sense that it provides a link between the Founding Generation and their own. A part of what the legal scholar Sanford Levinson has called our "constitutional faith"[26] surely turns on the popular belief that the Constitution of the present era is not radically discontinuous with the Constitution of the past—that constitutional change, in other words, has been gradual and predictable, rather than sharp and unexpected.[27] Thus the allegiance represented by obedience to courts is in some sense an allegiance to a particular narrative vision, one in which the judiciary, as it interprets the Constitution, is not making its principles up, but discovering them in the vision of the Framers. It does not matter whether smart scholars believe that the public perception is accurate; my only point is that the perception, if indeed it exists, should constrain rather than liberate the judiciary.

This is not to say that the act of interpretation is entirely mechanical. A machine, even one that would go of itself, could not do it. Constitutional interpretation is part science and part art. It is a creative act, yet one constrained by norms. The legal scholar Ronald Dworkin has likened it to writing a chain novel, in which each successive court adds a chapter that must be logically and artistically related to the previous one.[28] I would add that the metaphor of a novel works only as long as each writer remembers that the most important chapter to which the new addition must relate is chapter one—the original text. When this task is performed properly, it is, I would venture to say, an act of judicial allegiance: allegiance to the constitutional document, allegiance to a particular historical narrative, allegiance to the nation as a metaphor, and, most important, allegiance to the nation as a people—a people whose "repeated petitions" for redress the state that governs in their name ought never ignore.

Again, Religion and Interpretation

Let us consider how this interpretive proposition might work in practice. In the first lecture, I argued for a strong commitment to parental autonomy in the religious education of children—a commitment that is crucial if we believe in the freedom of religious communities to project their narrative traditions into the future. I mentioned at the time that although I am an agnostic on the subject of state support of private schools, I am quite certain that a program making aid available to some private schools but not to religious schools would be unconstitutional on its face. To see why, consider a city that has a rule providing that its fire department shall answer calls at any private building except a house of worship. The rationale for the rule is this: to put out a fire at a church or synagogue at public expense plainly furthers the religious mission of the congregation, if only by saving it a great deal of money. But to refuse to put out the fire on that ground would be a clear example of unconstitutional anti-religious discrimination.

The Supreme Court has been much criticized for its 1983

decision in *Mueller v. Allen*,[29] which upheld a Minnesota program of tax deductions for certain educational expenses, a program mostly used by parents whose children attended religious schools. According to critics of the decision—including the four dissenters—the program violated the wall of separation between church and state by granting aid to religious schools.[30] Now, in the first place, this would be an awkward interpretation of the First Amendment, since nearly every state at the time the amendment was adopted granted aid of some sort to at least some religions.[31] Far more important, however, the argument proves too much. If a tax deduction is state aid, and if aid to a religious school is unconstitutional, then a tax deduction that aids a religious organization directly must be even worse. So tax deductions for contributions to religious charities, to say nothing of churches and synagogues, as well as the tax exemption for the property religious groups own, would all be unconstitutional.

The critics of *Mueller* usually offer a simple distinction between aid to religious schools and aid to churches themselves: the special tax treatment of religious organizations recognizes that they perform important functions, such as charitable work, that the state itself would otherwise have to perform. In other words, the state may actually save money into the bargain. But this distinction is not even interesting. In the first place, I know of no other instance in which the argument that the government will save money, standing alone, is allowed to trump a constitutional prohibition. Besides, the religious schools, too, quite obviously perform functions that would otherwise be performed by the state. So, as it turns out, tax deductions for contributions to a religious organization are indistinguishable from tax deductions for tuition paid to religious schools—or, if one is constitutionally more suspect than the other, the villain is surely the deductibility of direct contributions.

Most important, to hold that the state cannot constitutionally provide even indirect support to parents who select religious schools for their children would be to break the historical narrative in a radical fashion. Even so hard-line a separationist as Leonard Levy, who argues strenuously against the constitutionality of aid to religious schools, concedes that at the time that the First Amendment was adopted, several states were supporting not just religious schools, but churches. Moreover, as we saw in the first lecture, the "public" schools with which the Framers were familiar, and those which existed during the nineteenth century, were essentially Protestant parochial schools. The first bill to grant federal aid to public schools was actually defeated on the ground that it did not include a provision for direct aid to the religious schools. In fact, as we have seen, nobody seriously argued that aid to religious schools was unconstitutional until the argument became a useful tool in the nativist campaign against Catholicism.

Now add to this history the simple facts that, first, most American parents whose children are in public schools wish they were in private religious schools and, second, most Americans support some form of direct or indirect government assistance to parents who choose religious schools. We can readily see the continuity between the parental desires of the present and the constitutional understanding of the past. We might, of course, forge a new understanding, under which all state aid to religious schools is unconstitutional, but the Supreme Court has wisely declined to press matters quite so far. On the contrary, in struggling to find a balance, the Justices seem to be acknowledging, albeit in fits and starts, that the constitutional narrative that would allow assistance is far better grounded in history than the narrative that would not. And this is a sensible course for a judicial branch that recognizes itself to be part of the sovereign and therefore is properly wary of repeatedly rejecting the repeated petitions of vast numbers of citizens.

Where does this leave us? It leaves us, among other places, with the hope that our judges, armed with a richer understanding of the Constitution, will perhaps respond more favorably to the "repeated petitions" of the dissenting religious parents whom we met in that first lecture, who are trying to preserve and nurture their traditions over time. Indeed, a court sensitive to history and context, understanding that traditions against state aid to parochial schools had their origins largely in anti-Catholic bigotry—and that the public schools themselves were created on a wave of religious sentiment—should not rush to reinforce the embarrassing message of our discriminatory history. The Justices were wise enough to avoid this trap when they decided in *Pierce*[32] that the state could not compel attendance at public schools: were parents not allowed to choose religious schools for their children, their traditions might well be destroyed. Although today's parents who fear the destruction of their traditions tend to be Protestants rather than Roman Catholics or Jews, the argument they are making is basically the same.

This suggests that we should be less constitutionally squeamish in the future than we have been in the past about allowing tax dollars to benefit the religions. The entire *Lemon v. Kurtzman*[33] tradition, under which the Supreme Court has constructed laborious rules for determining when aid to religious entities (including schools) is permissible, should be thrown out. And high time! For under the *Lemon* test, as it is so appropriately called, astonished and no doubt confused state officials have discovered that they are allowed to give parochial schools free textbooks but are not allowed to give them free maps. The test was too unruly to be managed even in its infancy and has grown only more unmanageable in its middle age.

What will we put in its place? A simple and unambiguous rule for understanding the religion clauses: except for the strongest of reasons, the state may not interfere with the religious liberty of its citizens. Some state practices—public school classroom prayer, for instance—would probably violate the rule, because of the obvious interference with the religious freedom of the family. But it is difficult to imagine a program of aid that would do so. The state would of course break the rule by showing favoritism to some religions over others and, in some circumstances, by favoring the religious over the non-religious. But the state would not break the rule by allowing religious organizations to take advantage of aid programs that secular groups are free to use. On the contrary: the only possible infringement on religious liberty would come if the churches were shut out.* And the American people would have to be thick indeed not to notice that their repeated petitions had been, once more, ignored.

Now, let me remind my listeners once again that I am by no means *advocating* state aid to religious schools. As I noted in the first lecture, I quite recognize that it might have unwanted ill effects. My argument is only that such aid is perfectly constitutional; and, further, that were the state to grant any aid at all to private schools, it would be unconstitutional to leave the religious schools out. Parents who choose religious educations for their children already sense the unfairness inherent in efforts to evade this basic constitutional truth; it remains to be seen whether the courts (and, I suppose, the scholars) will catch up.

Interpretation and Dissent

This would be the appropriate place to interpose a sharp objection: whatever the Court may properly consider, it should give

---

*After this lecture was delivered, the Small Business Administration abandoned its six-decade-old practice of refusing to allow religious organizations to obtain assistance. Under the rule proposed here, the SBA obviously did the right thing.

no weight to what the parents think. This weird sensitivity to public opinion is no proper part of judicial review.

But why shouldn't judges ever be sensitive to the possibility that their edicts will be disobeyed? In particular, why should they not consider the different interpretive positions held by outsiders—whether the "friends of the court" who file briefs or the editorial writers who play to their special audiences or even the politicians who give passionate speeches? One reason is history—as it happens, the same civil rights history we have been discussing in the past two lectures. The image of disobedience with which we are most familiar is doubtless of Governor Faubus standing in the schoolhouse door. But that history is of use only if we suppose it to prove that judges will usually be wiser than politicians. At times they are—but over the long run, the human beings who judge are every bit as capable of error and wickedness as the human beings who legislate or carry the laws into execution.

A second reason is that judicial consideration of the possibility of disobedience might violate the prescriptive rules of judging. In our hopeful rhetoric, we like to declare that judges decide on the basis of nothing but the facts before them and the statute, or perhaps constitutional clause, at issue. (This is why the rhetoric of "strict constructionism" used to play so well on the stump.) But we give the lie to this claim every time a vacancy opens on the Supreme Court and the various interest groups begin to maneuver to try to ensure that the nominee is forced, under oath, to pledge fealty to some particular constitutional vision—that is, to promise to vote a particular way.

Consider once more the classic example of the civil rights movement. As I mentioned, I believe the moral imperative represented by that movement to be the principal source of our antipathy toward judicial consideration of resistance to a decree. But the scope of what I have been meditating upon in these lectures—the dissent of the governed—is much broader, and I think it possible that the court decisions on school segregation do indeed signal the attention paid by the Justices to the possibility of disallegiance.

As a formal matter, *Brown v. Board of Education*[34] and the other desegregation cases that preceded it and followed it all represented interpretations of the equal protection clause of the Fourteenth Amendment. That clause provides that no state shall "deny to any person within its jurisdiction the equal protection of the laws." The classic pro-segregation argument was that because segregation laws keep white people away from black people as well as black people away from white people, they do not represent a denial of equal protection. This was the argument that the Supreme Court accepted in 1896, when it ruled, in *Plessy v. Ferguson*,[35] that segregation on streetcars did not violate this clause because the harm, if any, was only in the mind of the colored people who were raising the complaints. *Plessy* originated the phrase "equal but separate," which over the ensuing decades underwent a subtle transformation in emphasis and became "separate but equal."

But the *Brown* Court could not hide behind the mask of sociological jurisprudence that *Plessy* used. The reason was not that the Justices had a richer understanding of psychology, although they did. The reason, rather, goes back to the first lecture and the discussion of the Declaration of Independence. By 1954, when *Brown* was decided, it was clear to anybody who bothered to look that the nation's segregated and oppressed black folk had offered a long series of first plausible and at last morally imperative "repeated Petitions" which had been met only with "repeated injury." The political sovereign, at the local level but at the national level too, was ignoring the perfectly reasonable and often quite measured and respectful complaints of African America. After centuries of rebuff, black Americans might understandably have come to the conclusion that the nation had nothing to offer them—a dangerous conclusion for the rest of America. The nation might have been at grievous risk of metaphorical—or actual—revolution by those it was choosing to ignore and even punish.

The Justices stepped in, one might argue, in order to undo this grievous harm—in order to show black Americans that their "repeated Petitions" were being heard—and thereby to avoid providing a justification, in 1776 terms, for a massive act of disallegiance. And how did they step in? As only judges can, by finding a way, consistent with the prescriptive norms of judging but not dictated by them, to *interpret*—that's the key word—to *interpret* the words of the Fourteenth Amendment in a way that made racial segregation, which the Court had sustained just over half a century earlier, suddenly unconstitutional. And if, as I have argued, the legitimacy of a nation is measured ultimately by its treatment of dissenters, the Justices made a wise decision.

But the listener might once more object to this analysis, not of the case, but of proper judicial method. Surely the fact that somebody dissents cannot be sufficient reason to hold something unconstitutional, because every government act has its dissenters, and the government would thus be disabled from doing anything. Similarly, the listener might insist that the possibility of public dissent should never be even a part of the reason for refusing to hold something unconstitutional—that is, that judges should not hesitate to exercise their powers simply because of fear that their edicts will be disobeyed. After all, it can hardly be the function of the judiciary to make dissenters feel good, whether about the courts, about the country, or about themselves.

Remember, however, that the judges are a part of the sovereign, and as the courts share in the sovereign authority to make decisions, they also share in the sovereign responsibility not to allow dissent to spiral downward into disallegiance. The *Brown* Court, ironically, recognized this proposition twice: first, as we have seen, in 1954, when the Justices read the equal protection clause in a manner that was responsive to the repeated petitions of black Americans; and, second, in 1955, in declining to order the immediate desegregation of all schools,[36] perhaps, as some have argued, out of a fear of violent reaction by whites. Instead, the Court decided in *Brown II* to leave the matter to the discretion of the trial judges closest to the facts—and to the people. Even if *Brown II*'s "all deliberate speed" formula lacked the fine edge of logic that one would desire, judges who issue injunctions have always possessed broad power to tailor them to circumstances. And the principal circumstance to which the Justices evidently thought the desegregation injunctions should be tailored was the need to keep the peace.

Of course, the question of how to fashion a remedy is very different from the question of how to decide that a remedy is needed. One could sensibly conclude that whatever factors might influence the remedial stage of a litigation, the underlying question—*Who wins?*—should be decided without regard to popular opinion. In principle, this objection is correct. In practice, it is almost a non sequitur. As I noted earlier, if we as a people did not believe that our opinions *should* influence judges, we would not conduct confirmation hearings in a manner designed to elicit their promises to vote as we think best. If we as a people did not believe that our opinions *do* influence judges, we would not hold so many demonstrations around the Supreme Court.

In the fairly recent past, the Justices have evidently been at pains to let us know that they do not listen. For example, in the Court's 1992 *Casey* decision,[37] which allowed the states some greater leeway in regulating abortion, the four Justices who joined the principal opinion warned that any significant retreat from *Roe v. Wade*[38] would send the message that the Court is influenced by changes in the political climate. The warning itself, however, suggests that public activism *should* influence the Justices—if only by making them more steadfast. Indeed, the plurality opinion has a surreal, almost Wonderland aspect, in the implication that because of public protests against abortion, Justices who might otherwise be inclined to back away from *Roe*, even for perfectly legitimate analytical reasons, should instead stick with it. This, too, is a way of saying that popular opinion should influence constitutional interpretation.

I do not want to be read to suggest that judges should do what is popular, and I certainly do not mean that courts should be cowards. I am genuinely interested in the possible connection between the evolving constitutional understanding of the American people and what we might describe as the "correct" interpretation of a particular clause. So when I ponder whether a judge should take popular disagreement into account, I am not referring, in the manner of Alexander Bickel, to what the judge believes is prudent or wise. I am not concerned, therefore, with the metaphor of the courts as possessing scarce constitutional capital that they must decide whether to squander or save. Nor am I concerned, as judges sometimes must be, with the possibility that disobedience to a particularly unpopular decision might, through a mushroom effect, cause respect for law to vanish. I am concerned, rather, with the simple question of whether the judge got the answer right—whether the judge correctly applied the relevant interpretive norms to the relevant texts in the relevant contexts.

In this sense, my referent is the later Bickel—specifically, the Bickel who wrote *The Morality of Consent*, an extended essay on the role of the courts (and of protest) that was published shortly after his death. There Bickel described judicial review as an "endlessly renewed educational conversation" between the Supreme Court on the one hand and the public on the other.[39] In this, he anticipated the many later theorists who would envision judicial activity as essentially dialectical in nature. But Bickel did not mean simply that the Justices were to educate the people, for he admonished us to remember that his metaphor was of "a conversation not a monologue." Thus, for Bickel, the Justices must not merely talk but also listen.

Unless one considers the process of interpretation as mechanistic (an option we have already dismissed), or unless one believes that the courts are not a part of the sovereign, this approach is not only sensible but actually indispensable. Judicial review, like all governance, is indeed conversation, the more so in a democracy. The judicial half of the conversation involves the pronouncing of law; the public half involves the repeated petitions of which the Declaration spoke. When the lawgiving sovereign (no matter what the excuse) repeatedly ignores the petitions of the people whose allegiance provides its authority, dissent may indeed blossom into disallegiance.

And the people are not idiots. When judges, even constitutional judges, rely in large part on their own moral instincts in reaching their decisions, the fact can hardly be hidden: one can hardly claim, at this late date, that a decision like *Roe v. Wade* has secure foundation in much else. Relying on their own moral instincts already means that the judges are resting their interpretations in part on extra-constitutional sources of authority. Would it be so unreasonable for an aroused citizen—or an aroused majority of citizens—to wonder why the judges' moral instincts are a better extra-constitutional source than the moral instincts of the people themselves? Clearly not; nor can the judges themselves provide a persuasive response, unless the response indicates a willingness to engage in that conversation—not monologue—of which Bickel wrote.

But how is the judge who accepts this argument to avoid becoming a tool of the passing majority? The question answers itself. Judges (at least at the federal level) *do* have life tenure; they *do* possess a degree of independence from the popular will; so the only interesting issue is how they are to use such freedom as they hold. A sensitivity to the repeated petitions of the citizenry can certainly be balanced with the other, more usual norms of the judicial function, and the wisdom of judging comes in determining how the balance should best be struck. In the *Brown* litigation, the Supreme Court under Earl Warren probably produced the best balance possible. The embarrassing hubris of the current Court may make balance more difficult; if so, its edicts might, in the long run, contribute to the popular sense of a national sovereign that is out of control.

We are left, then, with two interpretive propositions: first, that a court that cares about the source of the obligation of the people to obey should be conscious of the need to link its work to a clear narrative that harks back to the Framing; and, second, that a court that cares about its role as part of the sovereign should be sensitive to the possibility that it might learn from the possibly quite distinct interpretive instincts of the public. The difficulty, obviously, is to find a way to make the two propositions work together. The talent of balancing the two is the mark of the exceptional jurist.

Consider a simple example in which our shared understanding—what most of us think is the most recent chapter of the novel, in Dworkin's metaphor—is sharply at odds with what the authors of the Constitution almost certainly had in mind—that is, the contents of chapter one. (Note that even here, I refer only to what people think is in the most recent chapter; I do not claim that many of us, no matter how strong our opinions on the matter, have actually taken the time to read it.) I have in mind the Establishment Clause of the First Amendment, the very beginning of the Bill of Rights, which reads: "Congress shall make no law respecting an establishment of religion." Ask most educated Americans what this language means, and they will tell you in an instant that it means that the government cannot establish religion. That belief is a commonplace of our political and social language. It is part of our legal language as well: every lawyer knows that the courts prohibit official "establishments" of religion, the effort that has led to the *Lemon* test and other efforts to determine when a particular official act "establishes" religion or not. Few constitutional principles (we tell ourselves in warm self-congratulation) are as firmly established.

But constitutional historians are aware of a different truth: the Establishment Clause was almost certainly designed for the single purpose of separating powers between the state and national sovereigns. The reason it begins "*Congress* shall make no law respecting an establishment of religion" is that the Framers feared only a *national* established religion. State establishments—several of which existed when the amendment was adopted—held no terror for the authors of the First Amendment. The amendment, in other words, was about the rights of the states, not about establishments of religion as such. On this understanding, the Supreme Court's 1947 *Everson* decision,[40] holding the states subject to the Establishment Clause, makes no analytical sense. As the legal scholar Akhil Amar has pointed out, the decision says in effect that a clause written to grant powers to the states actually takes it away.[41] To create an analogy at the state level to what the authors of the clause hoped to do would require the court to say, for example, that although the state of Connecticut, where I live, cannot establish a religion, the city of New Haven, where I work, can.

But even the most dedicatedly originalist jurist would understandably—and rightly—hesitate before declaring that state establishments of religion are perfectly fine. The reason for the hesitation would surely be our popular constitutional narrative, in which the state is not supposed to take sides on religious issues. Whether or not the Framers would have been troubled if tomorrow the state of Connecticut readopted the colonial legislation that forbade non-Christians to hold public office, most Americans would be appalled. We, the People of the United States, would consider the state's action unconstitutional. How does the fair judge balance this popular narrative, the recent chapters of Dworkin's chain novel, with the clear and very different understanding of the authors of the novel's first chapter? One possibility is to apply the underused Free Exercise Clause of the First Amendment to do much of the work that the overused Establishment Clause presently does. For example, as I noted in the first lecture, organized prayer in the public school classroom can readily be seen to violate the free exercise rights of families. But the Free Exercise Clause can be made to stretch only so far: as the legal scholar Michael McConnell has pointed out, to suggest that public tuition assistance to families who select parochial schools for their children violates the rights of those who choose public schools is a bit like saying that public funding for abortion services violates the rights of those who object.[42]

Indeed, a court that is sensitive to history and context, understanding that our narrative tradition against public aid to parochial schools had its birth largely in anti-Catholic bigotry, should not rush to reinforce that hateful message with a forced and implausible reading of the Establishment Clause—a reading that says to dissenting religious families who worry that their traditions may die that the sovereign does not, after all, hear their petitions. And so we wind up where we should be by now: back at the subject of the first lecture, armed with a reinterpreted Constitution to fit our reinterpreted Declaration of

Independence. We wind up with (hypothetical) judges who are sensitive to the need to avoid disallegiance, and so respond more favorably to the "repeated Petitions" of dissenting religious families, trying to project their traditions into the future, in the face of a legal and political climate often unsupportive of their efforts.

Now, bear in mind that my topic here is only interpretation—and that I am here offering only an example. So I am not actually advocating, as policy, public aid to religious schools. I am only explaining why such aid is not unconstitutional, or, more properly, why the tradition holding it unconstitutional is neither morally attractive nor historically defensible. And I am using that explanation to try to meet my own challenge, by integrating a theory of constitutional interpretation with a theory of political obligation. Naturally, there are many other ways to perform that integration, and some of them may prove more persuasive than the crude attempt made here. I am only insisting that once we understand the reinterpreted Declaration of Independence, we are forced to agree that the attempt itself matters.

You may naturally disagree with my effort to resolve the problem of the repeatedly rebuffed petitions of religious parents by reinterpreting the First Amendment. But do take note that today's religious freedom claimants (like the racial justice claimants of the previous generation) at least have bits of constitutional text on which to hang their petitions—which is more than one can say for many other claimants toward whom the courts sometimes demonstrate greater solicitude.

Or you may think my answer a little too pat. Perhaps it solves everything too neatly. Constitutional interpretation seems most realistic when it is a little bit grubby. So probably there is a better way to balance the clear and compelling contents of the first chapter of the First Amendment chain novel with the popular understandings of the last. But I do not pretend to have

found the best or the only answer; I do think that judges who are good at their work, and who understand that they are a part of, not separate from, the sovereign, are aware that this is the right question.

Conclusion: The Sovereign, the Courts, and Disallegiance

I suppose we have gone on long enough. Let me take a moment and review the path we have taken.

In the first lecture, I proposed rereading the Declaration of Independence in a way that places dissent rather than consent at the center of the question of the legitimacy of democratic government. I warned that our liberal constitutional ethos—by which I mean the tendency, common to political right and left alike, to assume that the nation must everywhere be morally the same—pressures citizens, across their wide variety, to be other than themselves, when being themselves would lead to disobedience. And I noted that the problem is particularly acute when the citizens happen to be religious, because it is in the nature of the religious citizen to try to form a community that will project into the future an understanding of the world that may be quite different from that of the sovereign majority of one's fellow citizens. Unfortunately, the project of liberal constitutionalism is to deny community autonomy by the force of law.

In the second lecture, I pointed out that our national history has not been friendly to the idea of civil disobedience, particularly disobedience in a religious cause, which might be described as part of the struggle to serve more than one master. Yet a democracy that believes in dialogue (as I hope we do) often achieves moral progress precisely through its ability to understand the motives and meanings of dissenters. Another way to put the point is that we need disobedience, and we should not be so quick to assume that disobedience is the same as disallegiance—although, to be sure, the quicker we are to dismiss and ridicule our disobedients, the quicker they will be to become what we might call disallegianists. And we need dissenting communities, both to blunt the power of the sovereign and to help us to move forward.

In the third lecture, I have been discussing the consequences of the first two lectures for the problem of constitutional interpretation. Although judges write as though they are outside the government, I have followed the Reverend Martin Luther King Jr.'s suggestion that courts are no different from any other part of the sovereign. Therefore, they share in the responsibility to uphold the dissenting tradition of the Declaration of Independence, and thus not to be too ready to rebuff the repeated petitions of angry citizens. This implies a judicial duty to give a degree of consideration to the public reception of their work, a perhaps heretical claim in this era of judicial popularity, but a perfectly sensible one if one believes that courts, too, govern.

In all of this, my concern has been for the autonomy of the many communities—particularly, but not exclusively, religious communities—into which democratic citizens organize themselves. That the mores of some of these communities may seem to be morally objectionable or simply bizarre only fortifies the point, for it is only through the willingness to accept these differences that we become truly democratic. The insistence that those who challenge accepted norms are challenging the sovereign itself is exactly what the Declaration of Independence was written against. Law, which has been the leveling tool of the project of liberal constitutionalism, should more properly serve as a means to preserve the diversity among our communities of meaning.

Perhaps my notion of community autonomy as the way to regain much-needed respect for the dissent of the governed will seem too radically discontinuous with the dominant single-national-community ethos of our era. I admit that I have no second solution. But it is wrong to do what we have always done, to find ways of forcing our dissenters into acts of disallegiance, so that we can treat them as criminals. True, there might have been other possibilities had we evolved in the second half of the twentieth century a more careful model of divided sovereignties, taking the states seriously as political entities, in the hope that unhappy citizens, ruled in part by an entity that seemed more within their reach than the distant, mysterious "Washington," would find mainstream politics more inviting.

But it could not have happened: racism poisoned any possibility. The awesome force of racial oppression, the bitterness with which it was nurtured, made inevitable the radical leaps in the authority of the national sovereign that we saw after the First Civil War in the 1860s and the Second Civil War a century after. Nowadays, whenever a problem needs solution, we imitate the civil rights model—a hefty centralized bureaucracy, backed up with uncompromising judges and well-armed troops—a choice that probably became inevitable, given our decision not to come face-to-face with our shared capacity for wickedness. For every time we say that *only* a nationwide solution enforced by the national sovereign can solve a problem— that *only* the rhetoric of critique that is appropriate for politics should be applied to every self-constituted community—and that *only* our own vision of constitutional meaning has any reality, a reality that must be universal—we are saying, in effect, that there is wickedness abroad but those of us who are able to reason and to influence the national sovereign do not share in it. We are saying that everyone else is the problem but we are the solution. We are saying that the millions of Americans who do not trust the national government are right not to trust it; they are right not to trust it because we *are* the national government, and we do not trust them.

That is not an attractive vision of democracy. It rejects the wisdom of the Declaration of Independence. Indeed, it may not be democracy at all. But it is the vision that centuries of racial oppression forced upon us. And in this era of devolution, challenged to surrender our exclusive claims of rightness, we are unable to do so. Public choice theory wins in the end: the ease with which we can influence a sovereign of concentrated power has become addictive, which no doubt helps explain why contemporary political theory focuses almost entirely on results rather than processes. There are no processes, or none that are significant; societal fairness, we now learn, must be judged purely by the output (in rights and entitlements) of a single central government that obsesses over making sure we treat each other right, having forgotten the lesson of the Enlightenment: what matters most in securing legitimacy is how the state treats *us*.

As I write these final words, the nation is arguing over devolution—the "return" of a degree of authority from the national government to the states. Liberals are sure it will be a disaster, conservatives are sure it will solve everything, and neither group has much basis for its certainty. I argued in the first lecture that we must be wary of geographic essentialism, the tendency to assume that everybody in a particular political subdivision shares a common interest, and I do not retreat from that critique. At the same time, I must confess that I understand the tug of devolution—the sense so many Americans would like to have of a government that is reachable, touchable, by ordinary folk. So it may be, under our reconstructed Declaration of Independence, that devolution is a good thing; perhaps even devolution past the state sovereigns to the local level, or devolution in moral and religious commitment, as is reflected in the accommodationist strain of Free Exercise jurisprudence that I have been discussing in this third lecture. Probably we should give devolution a try, less to be conservative than to be truly radical—to truly place power in the hands of people. For if in our self-satisfied certainty of our moral rightness we hesitate to devolve important choices even upon the state sovereigns, with all of their arbitrariness and weaknesses, we will never devolve them upon the multitudinous communities, whether we call them sovereigns or not, that provide our nation with its civic life. If instead we celebrate, always, results over people, bureaucracy over democracy, and centralization over community, then we are saying after all that we have no interest in the "repeated Petitions" of which the Declaration speaks, that we will, as our revolutionary forebears charged against George III, meet the petitions only with "repeated injury." If that is what constitutionalism has wrought, it is but one more sign that our celebration of the Declaration of Independence—indeed, our claim to democracy itself—is a sham.

Notes

Index

Notes

1. Allegiance

1. See Garry Wills, *Inventing America: Jefferson's Declaration of Independence* (Garden City, N.Y.: Doubleday, 1978), pp. 323–333.

2. For more on this story, see my book *Integrity* (New York: Basic Books, 1996), pp. 206–207.

3. For an explanation of my opposition to organized classroom prayer, see Stephen L. Carter, *The Culture of Disbelief: How American Law and Politics Trivialize Religious Devotion* (New York: Basic Books, 1993), pp. 184–192.

4. For an unfortunate example of this bias, from a scholar who should know better, see Amy Gutmann, *Democratic Education* (Princeton: Princeton University Press, 1987).

5. Margaret Farley, *Personal Commitments: Beginning, Keeping, Changing* (New York: Harper and Row, 1986), p. 44.

6. See, for example, *Communist Party of Indiana v. Whitcomb*, 414 U.S. 441 (1974), which rejected on free speech grounds a law requiring candidates for office to take a loyalty oath. Compare *Bond v. Floyd*, 385 U.S. 116 (1966), in which the Court ordered the Georgia legislature to seat Julian Bond, even though the state argued that Bond's antiwar rhetoric meant that he could not in good faith take the prescribed oath of membership.

7. Peter H. Schuck and Rogers M. Smith, *Citizenship without Consent: Illegal Aliens in America* (New Haven: Yale University Press, 1985).

8. George Fletcher makes this point in his excellent monograph entitled *Loyalty: An Essay in the Morality of Relationships* (New York: Oxford, 1993).

9. 410 U.S. 113 (1973).

10. See Ronald Dworkin, *Life's Dominion: An Argument about Abortion, Euthanasia, and Individual Freedom* (New York: Alfred A. Knopf, 1993), pp. 160–166.

11. 505 U.S. 833 (1992).

12. See *Immigration and Naturalization Service v. Chadha*, 462 U.S. 919 (1983).

13. 17 U.S. (4 Wheat.) 316 (1819).

14. Key decisions during the retreat include *NLRB v. Jones & Laughlin Steel Corp.*, 301 U.S. 1 (1937), and *United States v. Darby*, 312 U.S. 100 (1941).

15. See *United States v. Lopez*, 514 U.S. 549 (1995).

16. Richard Delgado and Jean Stefancic, "Imposition," *William and Mary Law Review* 35 (Spring 1994): 1025, 1056.

17. Just about a year after these lectures were delivered, the Supreme Court overturned the Colorado ordinance in *Romer v. Evans*, 116 S. Ct. 1620 (1996).

18. 488 U.S. 469 (1989).

19. Delgado and Stefancic, "Imposition," p. 1056.

20. 358 U.S. 1 (1958).

21. John R. Mulkern, *The Know-Nothing Party in Massachusetts: The Rise and Fall of a People's Movement* (Boston: Northeastern University Press, 1990), p. 30.

22. Another reason for the death of federalism may have been the emergence of the United States as a true military power in the wake of the First World War. In that conflict, a system of nationwide conscription replaced the traditional American process of raising regiments state-by-state. Thus, for the first time on any substantial scale, American armed forces fought for the nation as a whole rather than on behalf of their individual states.

23. Lani Guinier, "Groups, Representation, and Race-Conscious Districting: A Case of the Emperor's Clothes," *Texas Law Review* 71 (1993): 1589.

24. See David Tracy, *Plurality and Ambiguity: Hermeneutics, Religion, Hope* (New York: Harper and Row, 1987).

25. See Carter, *The Culture of Disbelief.*

26. See Alasdair MacIntyre, *After Virtue: A Study in Moral Theory*, 2nd ed. (South Bend: Notre Dame, 1984).

27. Samuel Fleischacker, *The Ethics of Culture* (Ithaca: Cornell University Press, 1994), p. 70. I also agree with Fleischacker that MacIntyre's view ultimately prevails.

28. Fletcher, *Loyalty*, p. 60.

29. See *Goldman v. Weinberger*, 475 U.S. 503 (1986).

30. See *Lyng v. Northwest Indian Cemetery Protective Association*, 485 U.S. 439 (1988).

31. 406 U.S. 205 (1972).

32. 512 U.S. 687 (1994).

33. 268 U.S. 510 (1925).

34. Compare *Board of Education v. Allen*, 392 U.S. 236 (1968) (okaying textbooks), with *Meek v. Pittenger*, 421 U.S. 349 (1975) (disallowing maps).

35. Warren A. Nord, *Religion and American Education: Rethinking a National Dilemma* (Chapel Hill: University of North Carolina Press, 1995).

36. United States Treasury Department [Alexander Hamilton], *Report of the Secretary of the Treasury of the United States: on the Subject of Manufactures* (Philadelphia: Childs and Swaine, 1791). The report was presented to the House of Representatives on December 5, 1791.

37. Humphrey J. Desmond, *The Know-Nothing Party* (Washington: New Century Press, 1905), p. 12.

38. See William Lee Miller, *The First Liberty: Religion and the American Republic* (New York: Knopf, 1986), p. 281.

39. Quoted in Desmond, *The Know-Nothing Party*, p. 54.

40. Thomas E. Bond, "The Know Nothings," in *The Wide-Awake Gift: A Know-Nothing Token for 1855* (New York: J. C. Derby, 1855), pp. 54, 55.

41. See Mulkern, *The Know-Nothing Party in Massachusetts*, p. 76.

42. H. Fuller, "Romanism," in *The Wide-Awake Gift*.

43. Michael F. Holt, *The Political Crisis of the 1850s* (New York: John Wiley and Sons, 1978), pp. 159–162.

44. See *Lemon v. Kurtzman*, 403 U.S. 602 (1971) (concurring opinion of Justice Douglas), p. 635, n. 20.

45. Horace Mann, "The Importance of Universal, Free, Public Education," quoted in Lawrence A. Cremin, ed., *The Republic and the School: Horace Mann on the Education of Free Men* (New York: Columbia University Teachers College, 1957), pp. 91–92.

46. See, for example, John Dewey, *Democracy and Education* (1916; New York: Macmillan, 1937).

47. Nord, *Religion and American Education*, p. 75.

48. Ibid., pp. 74–76.

49. See the discussion in Robert T. Handy, *Undermined Establishment: Church-State Relations in America, 1880–1920* (Princeton: Princeton University Press, 1991).

50. See Jay P. Dolan, *The American Catholic Experience: A History from Colonial Times to the Present* (Garden City, N.Y.: Doubleday, 1985).

51. Legal scholars, interestingly, have made this point. See, for example, the discussions in Douglas Laycock, "A Survey of Religious Liberty in the United States," *Ohio St. L. J.* 47 (1986): 409, and Phillip E. Johnson, "Concepts and Compromise in First Amendment Religious Doctrine," *Cal. L. Rev.* 72 (1984): 817.

52. Quoted in Steven C. Rockefeller, *John Dewey: Religious Faith and Democratic Humanism* (New York: Columbia, 1991), pp. 260, 267.

53. The legal scholar Stephen Gilles makes this point with some force in his stirring article "On Educating Children: A Parentalist Manifesto," *University of Chicago Law Review* 63 (1996): 937.

2. *Disobedience*

1. See, for example, Will Herberg, *Protestant-Catholic-Jew: An Essay in American Religious Sociology* (1955; Anchor Books, 1960); and Jeremy Rabkin, "Disestablished Religion in America," *Public Interest* 86 (1987): 124.

2. This argument should not be taken to mean that I oppose the ordination of women. On the contrary, I support it, on scriptural grounds that I have discussed in other writing. See Stephen L. Carter, *The Culture of Disbelief: How American Law and Politics Trivialize Religious Devotion* (New York: Basic Books, 1993), pp. 75–80. But I do not believe that one must be a sexist in order to disagree with my interpretations of God's Word.

3. See, for example, Frederick Mark Gedicks, *The Rhetoric of Church and State: A Critical Analysis of Religion Clause Jurisprudence* (Durham, N.C.: Duke University Press, 1995); and Michael W. McConnell, "Religious Freedom at a Crossroads," *University of Chicago Law Review* 59 (1992): 115.

4. 98 U.S. 145 (1879).

5. 494 U.S. 872 (1990).

6. Ibid., p. 890.

7. 406 U.S. 205 (1972).

8. The Religious Freedom Restoration Act was declared unconstitutional in *City of Boerne v. Flores*, 521 U.S. — (1997). Although I think this decision was a very bad one, many thoughtful scholars certainly predicted it. See, for example, Marci A. Hamilton, "The Religious Freedom Restoration Act: Letting the Fox into the Henhouse under Cover of Section 5 of the Fourteenth Amendment," *Cardozo Law Review* 16 (Dec. 1994): 357; and Christopher L. Eisgruper and Lawrence G. Sager, "Why the Religious Freedom Restoration Act Is Unconstitutional," *New York University Law Review* 69 (1994): 437.

9. See, for example, Justice Thomas's dissent from denial of certiorari in *Swanner v. Anchorage Equal Rights Commission*, 513 U.S. 979 (1994). The case involved a property owner charged with violating state and local ordinances prohibiting discrimination by landlords on the basis of marital status. The owner refused to rent to an unmarried couple because of "his sincere religious belief that such cohabitation is a sin and that he would be facilitating the sin by renting to cohabitants." Ibid., p. 460. When the

owner claimed that the Religious Freedom Restoration Act prohibited the state from punishing him for his religiously motivated refusal to rent, the Alaska Supreme Court found that the state had a compelling interest in enforcing its ordinance. Justice Thomas pointed out that the state of Alaska could not genuinely believe the interest in avoiding marital-status discrimination compelling, because the state itself reserved some benefits for married couples that others did not receive. He went on to say this: "If, despite affirmative discrimination by Alaska on the basis of marital status and a complete absence of any national policy against such discrimination, the State's asserted interest in this case is allowed to qualify as a 'compelling' interest—that is, a 'paramount' interest, an interest 'of the highest order'—then I am at a loss to know what asserted governmental interests are not compelling. The decision . . . drains the word compelling of any meaning and seriously undermines the protection for exercise of religion that Congress so emphatically mandated in RFRA." Ibid., p. 462. But, of course, legal scholars have long understood (but too rarely been frightened by) the power of the courts to use interpretation to rid themselves of inconvenient statutes.

10. Martin Luther King, Jr., "Letter from Birmingham City Jail," in James M. Washington, ed., *A Testament of Hope: The Essential Writings of Martin Luther King, Jr.* (San Francisco: Harper and Row, 1986), pp. 294.

11. See *Texas v. Johnson*, 491 U.S. 397 (1989).

12. *Gitlow v. New York*, 268 U.S. 652 (1925).

13. Robert Justin Goldstein, *Political Repression in Modern America: From 1870 to the Present* (Cambridge, Mass.: Schenkman, 1978), p. 487.

14. 403 U.S. 15 (1971).

15. The reasons for this disbelief I detail, with perhaps too much heat, in Stephen L. Carter, *Reflections of an Affirmative Action Baby* (New York: Basic Books, 1991).

16. I discuss this proposition in Stephen L. Carter, "The Black Table, the Empty Seat, and the Tie," in Gerald Early, ed., *Lure and Loathing: Essays on Race, Identity, and the Ambivalence of Assimilation* (Penguin, 1993), p. 64.

17. Regina Austin, " 'An Honest Living': Street Vendors, Municipal Regulation, and the Black Public Sphere," *Yale Law Journal* 103 (1994): 2119.

18. Ibid.

19. See *Lyng v. Northwest Indian Cemetery Protective Association*, 485 U.S. 439 (1988), p. 451.

20. Martin Buber, "Dialogue," in *Between Man and Man*, tr. Ronald Gregor Smith (New York: Macmillan, 1965), pp. 1, 7. The essay was first published in 1929.

21. Compare Michael Walzer, *Spheres of Justice: A Defense of Pluralism and Equality* (New York: Basic Books, 1983), using a similar metaphor to make a related but somewhat different point.

22. See Pope John Paul II, *The Gospel of Life: On the Value and Inviolability of Human Life* (Washington: United States Catholic Conference, 1995), pp. 131-137.

23. The late Robert Cover helped introduce this point to legal analysis. See, for example, Robert M. Cover, "Violence and the Word," *Yale Law Journal* 95 (1986): 1601.

24. Paul Johnson, *A History of Christianity* (New York: Atheneum, 1976), p. 456.

25. See *Dambrot v. Central Michigan University*, 839 F. Supp. 477 (E.D. Mich. 1993); *UVM Post, Inc. v. Board of Regents of University of Wisconsin System*, 774 F. Supp. 1163 (E.D. Wis. 1991); and *Doe v. University of Michigan*, 721 F. Supp. 852 (E.D. Mich. 1989).

26. I borrow this comparison from Michael McConnell. See his "The Selective Funding Problem: Abortions and Religious Schools," *Harvard Law Review* 104 (1991): 989.

27. Pope John Paul II, *The Gospel of Life*, pp. 12, 134.

28. See Albert O. Hirschman, *Exit, Voice, and Loyalty* (Cambridge, Mass.: Harvard University Press, 1990).

29. See generally Joel Feinberg, *The Moral Limits of the Criminal Law*, vol. 2, *Offense to Others* (New York: Oxford, 1985).

30. See Gedicks, *The Rhetoric of Church and State;* Angela Carmella, "A Theological Critique of Free Exercise Jurisprudence," *George Washington Law Review* 60 (1992): 782; and Michael W. McConnell, "Accommodation of Religion: An Update and a Response to the Critics," *George Washington Law Review* (1992): 685, 738-741.

31. 410 U.S. 113 (1973).

32. Ronald M. Dworkin, *Life's Dominion: An Argument about Abortion, Euthanasia, and Individual Freedom* (New York: Knopf, 1993).

33. For the fullest version of this argument, see Michael Tooley, *Abortion and Infanticide* (Oxford: Clarendon, 1983).

34. Pope John Paul II, *The Gospel of Life*, pp. 133, 136 (emphasis in original).

35. *Walker v. City of Birmingham*, 388 U.S. 307 (1967).

3. Interpretation

1. See *Walker v. City of Birmingham*, 388 U.S. 307 (1967).
2. 358 U.S. 1 (1958).

3. Martin Luther King, Jr., "Letter from Birmingham City Jail," in James M. Washington, ed., *A Testament of Hope: The Essential Writings of Martin Luther King, Jr.* (San Francisco: Harper and Row, 1986), p. 36.

4. *Walker*, pp. 320–321.

5. Only Justice John Marshall Harlan, in his separate opinion in *Shuttlesworth v. City of Birmingham*, 394 U.S. 147 (1969), seemed to understand the significance to the marchers of holding a protest on Good Friday. See ibid., pp. 159–164.

6. 418 U.S. 683 (1974).

7. *United States v. Burr*, 25 F. Cas. 187 (C.C. Va. 1807).

8. See Arthur Leff, "Law and," *Yale Law Journal* 87 (1978): 989.

9. See Alexander Bickel, *The Least Dangerous Branch: The Supreme Court at the Bar of Progress* (New Haven: Yale University Press, 1962).

10. 71 U.S. (4 Wall.) 475 (1867).

11. 98 U.S. 145 (1879).

12. 494 U.S. 872 (1990).

13. *Employment Division v. Smith*, 494 U.S. 872, 890 (1990).

14. George Fletcher, *Loyalty: An Essay on the Morality of Relationships* (New York: Oxford University Press, 1993), p. 44.

15. See William H. Rehnquist, *Grand Inquests: The Historic Impeachments of Justice Samuel Chase and President Andrew Johnson* (New York: Morrow, 1992), ch. 4.

16. The Rosenbergs raised a last-minute constitutional challenge claiming that although the crime for which they had been convicted was called espionage, it was the same crime that the Framers contemplated in crafting the Constitution's definition of treason, and should therefore be subject to the same strictures on witnesses and overt acts. See the discussion in Fletcher, *Loyalty*, p. 48.

17. A useful, if unusual, retelling of the Zenger story is Eben Moglen, "Considering Zenger: Partisan Politics and the Legal Profession in Provincial New York," *Columbia Law Review* 94 (1994): 1495.

18. James W. Ely, Jr., "The Chicago Conspiracy Case," in Michael R. Belknap, ed., *American Political Trials* (Westport, Conn.: Greenwood Press, 1994), pp. 233, 245.

19. See the discussion in Stephen L. Carter, *Integrity* (New York: Basic Books, 1996), pp. 171–181.

20. Compare Bruce Ackerman, *We, the People: Foundations* (Cambridge, Mass.: Belknap/Harvard, 1991).

21. See, for example, the elegant discussion in Robert M. Cover, "*Nomos* and Narrative," *Harvard Law Review* 97 (1983): 4, esp. pp. 40–44.

22. See *Cantwell v. Connecticut*, 310 U.S. 296 (1940).

23. See Stephen L. Carter, *The Culture of Disbelief: How American Law and Politics Trivialize Religious Devotion* (New York: Basic Books, 1993), chs. 7, 8.

24. One may come to the same point from an entirely different direction. Consider the following argument: the courts, especially in religious freedom cases concerning faiths of which they know little, should struggle toward *humility* rather than *hubris*—that is, they should be wary of believing in their own infallibility, notably when enunciating or interpreting broad principles of justice. Thus, as the former federal judge Marvin Frankel points out in a recent book, it is one thing to convict the Reverend Jim Bakker of fraud after he lied in his fundraising, both about how many "lifetime partnerships" in his "Heritage Village" he would be selling and about what he would do with the money. Committing fraud is an easy case: notwithstanding the religious content of his behavior, Bakker deserved to go to jail. But do we really want the courts inquiring into which expenditures of the Unification Church are for religious purposes and which are not, as the judge and jury did in convicting the Reverend Sun Myung Moon of filing false tax returns? Scores of religious and civil libertarian groups that agree on nothing else supported Moon, and small wonder: inquiry of that kind, by an arm of the state, risks forcing all religions into a particular mold—dare we say an American Protestant mold?—which hardly seems consistent with anybody's ideal of religious freedom. See Marvin E. Frankel, *Faith and Freedom: Religious Liberty in America* (New York: Hill and Wang, 1994).

25. Michael G. Kammen, *A Machine That Would Go of Itself: The Constitution in American Culture* (New York: Knopf, 1986).

26. See Sanford Levinson, *Constitutional Faith* (Princeton: Princeton University Press, 1988).

27. I discuss this proposition in more detail in Stephen L. Carter, "Constitutional Adjudication and the Indeterminate Text: A Preliminary Defense of an Imperfect Muddle," *Yale Law Journal* 94 (1985): 821, and in an unpublished lecture entitled "The Immutable Constitution," which was delivered at the University of Pennsylvania Law School.

28. See, for example, Ronald Dworkin, *Law's Empire* (Cambridge, Mass.: Belknap/Harvard, 1986), pp. 228–232, and elsewhere.

29. 463 U.S. 388 (1983).

30. See, for example, the very thoughtful argument against "nonpreferential assistance" to religious schools in Leonard W. Levy, *The Establishment Clause: Religion and the First Amendment* (New York: Macmillan, 1986). For my reaction to Levy, see *The Culture of Disbelief*, ch. 10.

31. For a brisk discussion of this history, see Arlin M. Adams and Charles J. Emmereich, *A Nation Dedicated to Religious Liberty: The Consti-*

tutional Heritage of the Religion Clauses (Philadelphia: University of Pennsylvania Press, 1990).

32. *Pierce v. Society of Sisters*, 268 U.S. 510 (1925). The case is discussed in greater detail in the first lecture.

33. 403 U.S. 602 (1971).

34. 347 U.S. 483 (1954).

35. 163 U.S. 537 (1896).

36. See *Brown v. Board of Education*, 349 U.S. 294 (1955). This case is usually referred to as *Brown II*.

37. *Planned Parenthood of Southeastern Pennsylvania v. Casey*, 505 U.S. 833 (1992).

38. 410 U.S. 113 (1973).

39. Alexander Bickel, *The Morality of Consent* (New Haven: Yale University Press, 1975), p. 111.

40. *Everson v. Board of Education*, 330 U.S. 1 (1947).

41. See Akhil R. Amar, "The Bill of Rights as a Constitution," *Yale Law Journal* 100 (1991): 1131, 1157–61.

42. See Michael W. McConnell, "The Selective Funding Problem: Abortions and Religious Schools," *Harvard Law Review* 104 (1991): 989.

Index

for the autonomy of communities—especially but not exclusively religious—into which democratic citizens organize themselves as a condition for dissent, dialogue, and independence. With reference to a number of cases, Carter shows that disobedience is sometimes necessary to the heartbeat of our democracy—and that the distinction between challenging accepted norms and challenging the sovereign itself, a distinction crucial to the Declaration of Independence, must be kept alive if we are to progress and prosper as a nation.

STEPHEN L. CARTER is William Nelson Cromwell Professor of Law at Yale Law School and the author of *The Culture of Disbelief: How American Law and Politics Trivialize Religious Devotion*.

The William E. Massey Sr. Lectures in the History of American Civilization

HARVARD UNIVERSITY PRESS
CAMBRIDGE, MASSACHUSETTS
LONDON, ENGLAND
www.hup.harvard.edu